The Trout and Salmon Fisherman's Bible

The
Trout and Salmon
Fisherman's
Bible

James L. Bashline

DOUBLEDAY
NEW YORK   LONDON   TORONTO   SYDNEY   AUCKLAND

PUBLISHED BY DOUBLEDAY
a division of Bantam Doubleday Dell Publishing Group, Inc.
666 Fifth Avenue, New York, New York 10103

DOUBLEDAY and the portrayal of an anchor with a
dolphin are trademarks of Doubleday, a division of
Bantam Doubleday Dell Publishing Group, Inc.

Library of Congress Cataloging-in-Publication Data

Bashline, James L.
    The trout and salmon fisherman's bible / James L. Bashline.
        p.   cm.
    1. Trout fishing.   2. Salmon-fishing.   I. Title.
SH687.B377   1991   91-10424
799.1′755—dc20   CIP

Contents

1

Introduction to Trout and Salmon

There are trout of some kind on every continent in the world. Salmon are not quite so widely distributed, but efforts to transplant them have been successful in a number of places. When the British Union Jack flew over many of the remote corners of the globe, the trout of the British Isles, namely the brown trout, was introduced to many foreign waters. Browns flourished in New Zealand, Australia, Tasmania, Ceylon, and the mountainous countries of southern Africa. And, of course, the introduction of the German brown trout to North America was an amazing success.

The biological game of "musical chairs" with Salmonidae, the family under which trout and salmon are classified, worked in reverse as well. Rainbow and brook trout, natives of the New World, made trips to Europe, South America, the down-under countries, and heaven knows where else. There are even rainbow trout in a few mountain streams in Costa Rica, where they live in harmony with monkeys and parrots. Indeed, trout and salmon are available to a huge slice of the world's anglers.

Wherever they exist, trout enjoy a high posi-

tion on the angling status ladder. They are handsome, crafty fishes; they reproduce well in suitable water, and they are among the finest of table fare. No wonder more words have been written about them than about any other group of fish.

BROOK TROUT
(*Salvelinus fontinalis*)

This is the trout of the American Northeast, of the Appalachians and eastern Canada. As we move into the northern habitat of this beautiful fish, it usually assumes larger proportions. A "trophy" brook trout in the hills of Tennessee, for example, would be no more than 12 inches long, whereas it would take a brookie of 4 pounds or more to raise eyebrows in the wilderness regions of Labrador or Quebec. The reasons are threefold: food supply, longevity, and angling pressure. The brook trout, wherever it's found and in whatever size range, is among the easiest of all trout to catch . . . if the angler is reasonably cautious.

The brook trout is the native fish of many eastern streams and lakes with suitably cold water. Once unknown west of the Rocky Mountains, it has been transplanted to several western states.

Range of the brook trout.

The brook trout has much smaller scales than other trout or salmon and lacks some of their features, notably the vomerine bone in the upper jaw. But this is of little consequence to the angler.

Identifying the brook trout is relatively easy if the angler remembers two basic clues. The brook trout has *no* black spots and wears some wormlike markings on its back called vermiculations. On some fish these wiggly marks are less distinctive, but they can usually be seen. The brookie also has distinctive fins edged in lines of black and white. These edges become more prominent as the fish approach spawning season during the autumn months. Their bellies and the major portion of the fins take on a reddish hue that is amazingly brilliant. Red spots on halos of blue are also brookie trademarks, particularly along the lateral lines.

A trophy brook from eastern Canada. It takes a long time to grow a brookie this large. Today, most of these big fish are released. This one hit a popping bug.

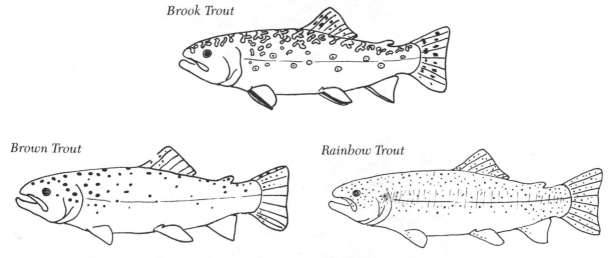

Brook Trout

Brown Trout

Rainbow Trout

Trouts and chars can be identified by their spots. The brook trout has vermiculations, or "turkey tracks," on the back with no black spots. The brown has dark brown to black spots with some red spots along the lateral line. The rainbow has a pinkish or red mid-stripe with black spots only.

BROWN TROUT
(*Salmo trutta*)

Of all the creatures that have been brought to North America, the brown trout is the most important. It arrived at a most opportune time, the late 19th century. At that moment in history, the protective canopy of large trees was being removed from eastern forests at an alarming rate. This raised the water temperatures in many rivers and made life difficult for the eastern brook trout, which requires slightly colder water in order to spawn and thrive, but didn't bother the brown trout, which can tolerate warmer water. Thus, the brownie has provided excellent fishing for over a century in nearly every state in the nation and in many other countries as well.

Although the British are responsible for transporting the brown trout to other lands, they did not, curiously, bring the first brown trout to America. It has long been widely accepted that an early fish culturalist named Fred Mather raised the first browns released in the United States from eggs purchased in Germany. The year was 1883. It now appears that there was an earlier shipment of brown trout eggs from the Netherlands to John P. Creveling, of Allentown, Pennsylvania, some years before. The Marietta Hatchery, the first in Pennsylvania, was managed by Creveling, and his diaries and state records show that brown trout were being raised there when the hatchery closed in 1883. *Note*: This information was supplied by Wilbur C. Creveling, Jr., grandson of John, and is corroborated by existing Pennsylvania Fish Commission records.

As the years passed, more brown trout from Germany, England, Scotland, and probably other countries as well found their way to America, and the brownie became a highly respected citizen. The adaptability of the brown to a wide variety of water chemistry and type is one of the

A 3-pound brown trout from a Utah river. This is how to cradle a fish that is to be released without hurting it.

Heavily spotted brown trout being correctly led head first into the landing net. It struck a small dry fly.

reasons for its popularity. It flourishes in huge lakes, pocket-size ponds, and rivers of all sizes—as long as there is flowing water in which to drop its eggs. It grows well on a wide variety of foods, including insects, baitfish, crustaceans, and other water- and land-born creatures. In some rivers which empty into saltwater, brown trout go to sea for a feeding period just as salmon do and become as silvery as a new coin. Brown trout are the sea trout of Europe, Iceland, and more recently of the southern tip of South America.

The fly fishermen of the world, particularly those in the United Sates, have benefited most from the brown trout. The hardy European fish is fond of aquatic insects, especially the mayflies that appear in spring and summer. These protein-rich insects offer easy pickings for the surface-feeding brown as they drift along during a hatch. For a growing number of anglers, cast-

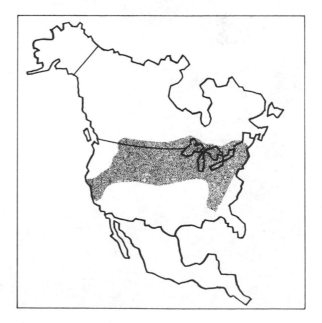

Range of the brown trout.

ing dry flies over rising brown trout is the apex of angling.

Because of the mixed brown trout strains in hatcheries and in the wild as well, making a pronouncement about the coloration or other physical characteristics of all brown trout is problematical. Compounded by outside factors such as overhead shade, depth of water, available food, and some we don't know about, brown trout can vary from dark brown to steely-gray and any color in between. Tiny browns from mountain streams can be nearly solid black on their backs and as brilliant as brook trout on the flanks. Conversely, football-fat browns from one of the Great Lakes can be as silvery as a new nickel. But the chief clue to identification is the color of the spots. Brown trout have black, dark brown, and often red spots (whereas brook trout have *no* black spots). The bellies and fins of many brown trout favor yellow with a tinge of red during the fall spawning seasons. The adipose fin (the little one in front of the tail) is sometimes spotted and occasionally solid red or brown. It is

not unusual to see an edge of white on the ventral and anal fins of browns found in steams. On larger fish, those over 18 inches long, a few spots may appear on the upper and lower edges of the tail.

RAINBOW TROUT
(*Oncorhynchus mykiss*)*

The rainbow trout is primarily a fish of the Pacific drainage system. It is found in many western lakes and streams that do not have access to

*Taxonomists have recently agreed to recognize the trouts of the northern Pacific drainages as being more closely allied with Pacific salmon. Therefore, the scientific names appearing in this text may seem unfamiliar to some readers. As with previous name changes, several years will pass before the new names become common.

The species affected by these name changes are: Apache trout becomes *Oncorhynchus apache*, cutthroat trout becomes *O. clarki*, Gila trout becomes *O. gilae*, golden trout becomes *O. aguabonita* and rainbow trout becomes *O. mykiss*. The genus name, Oncorhynchus, is pronounced *on-core-inkus*. Common names will remain unchanged.

Ranbow trout usually have black spots, and this 2½-pound fish is no exception. If held gently in this manner trout can be easily unhooked.

the ocean, but it's probably a safe guess that they once did. The rainbows that head for the ocean after spawning are known as steelheads or steelhead trout and are one and the same. This has long presented a problem in stocking rainbow trout, because some rainbows never lose their taste for saltwater. Selective breeding in hatcheries has reduced this tendency to a great extent, and we now have rainbow trout in nearly every state, province, and country that boasts of trout fishing. They are almost as adaptable as the brown trout in accepting new homes. They are widely distributed in the eastern United States, as they grow fast in hatcheries for stocking purposes and can survive in water that is too warm for brook trout. The rainbow has been a big success in British lakes and is widely distributed in Chile and Argentina.

Unlike the browns and brooks, the rainbow is

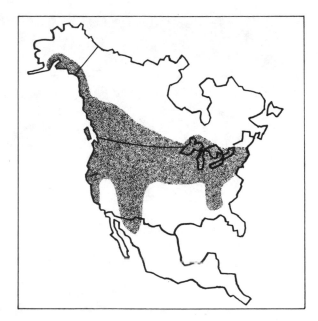

Range of the rainbow trout.

A 12-pound rainbow trout from a mountain stream in Chile, perfectly formed and in its prime.

predominantly a late winter or early spring spawner. In rivers and small brooks it prefers faster water than the other trout species, but it also adapts easily when forced to live in large lakes where it quickly becomes an active minnow eater. The most famous attribute of the rainbow trout is its inclination to leap when hooked, making it an exciting fish to catch. Brook trout jump infrequently and browns occasionally.

The most recognizable cosmetic feature of the rainbow trout is the pink or reddish swath extending from the gill cover along the fish's side. During the spring spawning season this stripe can be brilliant, while at other times it is quite pale. Upon entering freshwater, the steelhead variety of rainbow is silver on the flanks and steely-gray on the back and halfway down the flank to the lateral line. The pink stripe returns as the fish spends more time in the river, with the male's being much more pronounced than the female's.

Rainbows that spend their entire lives in freshwater are almost always heavily marked from head to tail with spots ranging from the size of a pea to mere pepper flakes. All of the spots on

A husky, beautifully marked rainbow from Alaska, a wild, stream-born fish. With catch-and-release regulations now in force on many rivers, the future looks good for Alaskan rainbows.

Steelhead trout are decidedly dark on the back and silvery on the sides, with a pronounced line separating the gradation. This is more prominent when the fish have just returned from the sea.

a rainbow are black. They wear no red spots nor do they sport the blue halos of the brookie.

CUTTHROAT TROUT
(*Oncorhynchus clarki*)

This is the native trout of the Rocky Mountains. Its range extends well beyond those peaks, however, and strains of cutthroats can be found in Mexico and many parts of western Canada and Alaska. For some reason, cutthroats have not been successfully transplanted in the eastern half of North America nor abroad. The cutthroats liking for very cold water and their tendency to interbreed with rainbows may be the limiting factors. Regardless, it's the fish of the cowboy states and a beautiful thing it is. The cutthroat is a ready eater and is especially fond of

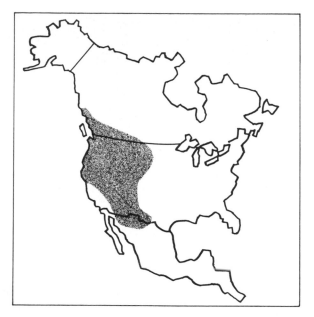

Range of the cutthroat trout.

This cutthroat trout fell for a tiny dry fly. Fewer spots and a red or orange slash mark at the throat identify this handsome trout of the West Coast and the Rockies.

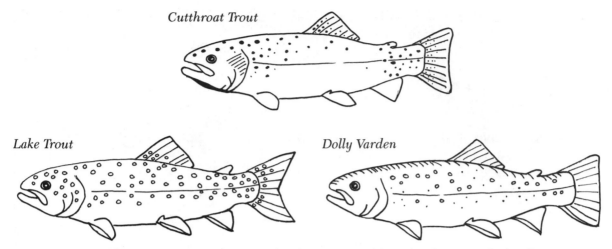

Cutthroat Trout

Lake Trout

Dolly Varden

Cutthroat trout are easily identified by the red slash at the throat, pinkish gill covers, and absence of a red stripe along the flank. The lake trout has plenty of cream-colored spots from head to tail and a more deeply forked tail than other char or trout. The Dolly Varden has whitish and red spots, and white-edged fins in many waters.

underwater nymphs and other aquatic creatures. It comes well to all sorts of sunken lures and flies and will rise as freely as any trout to a hatch of surface insects.

Identifying the cutthroat can be a bit tricky in waters where rainbows also live. Since the two fish do interbreed, there is the variable of the "cross" fish. A pure strain cutthroat always has a reddish or orange slash on the bottom of each gill cover that shows more prominently as the mouth is opened. In some fish this slash is wide and almost artificially red. Its flanks may be silvery or yellowish with more red on the gill covers and forepart of the body. The back varies from olive to brown. There are usually spots from head to tail, not as many as on the rainbow, but they are larger, especially toward the tail.

Like most trouts and chars, some cutthroats spend feeding time in the Pacific Ocean if they have access and there they take on the silvery sheen that marks them as sea-run fish.

LAKE TROUT
(*Salvelinus namaycush*)

The lake trout is the big daddy of the North American trouts and chars. It is closely related to the brook trout (also a char) and interbreeds with that species. The cross is known as a splake. Lake trout weighing over 100 pounds have been caught in commercial nets. Fifty-pounders are caught each year in several Canadian lakes and 30-pounders are becoming common once more in the Great Lakes and a few other waters.

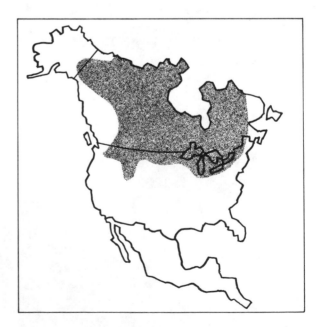

Range of the lake trout.

Three- and 4-pound lake trout take flies greedily soon after ice-out and provide
great sport on a fly rod. Note the deeply forked tails.

Preferring deep, cold water, the lake trout, also known as togue or mackinaw in some locales, is usually caught while trolling or with deep jigging tackle. These fish cruise near the surface in the early spring and late fall months—but not for long. Their liking for water below 50 degrees F keeps them deep most of the time. While deep lakes are their usual habitat, lake trout also can be found in flowing water when they're spawning or if the water temperature remains cool. In some arctic and near arctic rivers, such as those that flow into Ungava Bay in Quebec, big lakers are plentiful.

Spots are again the key to identifying a lake trout. They are usually light gray to yellowish cream on a darker gray to silvery background. While the pattern of the spots varies from region to region, this general overall marking layout is quite consistent. The tail is forked—that is, it has a deep "V" that is unlike that of other chars or trouts. On many lake trout the leading edge of the under fins is rimmed with a line of cream or white and a corresponding black line. These lines are more prominent at spawning time. In some waters the fins show hints of red or yellow.

DOLLY VARDEN
(*Salvelinus malma*)

This western char is common to Pacific drainage waters and inland to Montana, where it's more commonly referred to as "bull trout." Because it feeds heavily on small salmon or on any other small fish for that matter, it has long been considered less than desirable. This feeling is passing with good reason: the Dolly Varden is a fine game fish and provides excellent sportfishing where there might not be any otherwise. The Dolly is a long-lived fall spawner that grows to prodigious

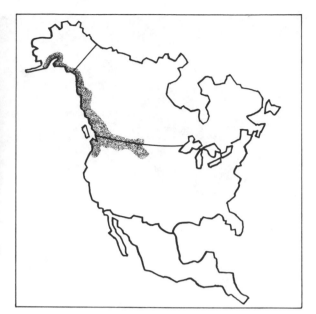

Range of the Dolly Varden.

Dolly Varden are fish of the West Coast and inland to Montana. They are also known as bull trout in some regions. The Dolly is a char; its large creamish spots distinguish it from the true trout.

compounded. Dolly Vardens have red spots in some waters, particularly those that do not lead to the ocean. Some fish in deeper lakes have pale yellow spots and few, if any, red spots. They never have black spots. Generally, if the spots are smaller than the end of a pencil eraser it's a Dolly Varden; if larger, it's an Arctic char. The sides and bellies can take on a pronounced pinkish or reddish hue just before the spawning season, and some of them even show the vermiculations seen on eastern brook trout.

ARCTIC CHAR
(*Salvelinus alpinus*)

As the name implies, this is a northern cold-water fish whose range nearly rims the top of the world. It is found in landlocked form in a few northern countries, but is usually thought of as a sea-run fish through most of its range. Canada, Russia, Norway, and Alaska have most of the Arctic char, with Canada having the lion's share. Arctic char are found there from Labrador north to Baffin Island and then west to the Northwest Territories. In Quebec and northeastern Canada

size in some waters. Fifteen and 20-pounders are not uncommon in large lakes and rivers.

Where Dolly Vardens have access to saltwater, many of them spend feeding time there just as salmon, trout, and other char do. They wax fat in the ocean and return as sleek and silvery as any other anadromous fish. And here we have a most difficult identification problem.

It's easy to confuse a sea-run Dolly with an Arctic char. If Dollies were common in waters frequented by sea-run brook trout (that's a char too, remember) the problem would really be

Arctic Char

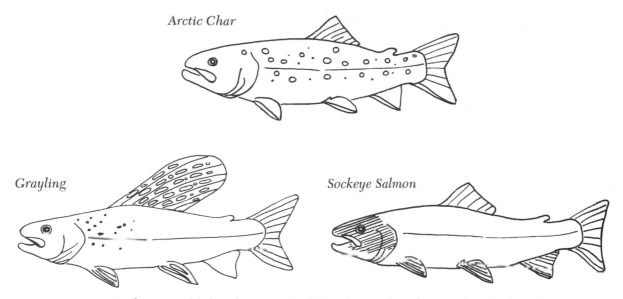

Grayling

Sockeye Salmon

Arctic char resemble brook trout or Dolly Vardens and can be mistaken for them. They are found farther north than the other chars and usually are a sea-run species. They are very silvery when they enter spawning rivers, but the males quickly become highly colored with crimson sides.

there are strains of inland char, as there are in Norway and Siberia.

Opinions differ, of course, but the Arctic char is arguably the most spectacularly colored of any

Range of the Arctic char.

A husky Arctic char from an Alaskan river.

fish in the world when displaying its spawning colors. Like all sea-run fish, this char is silvery and sleek as it enters freshwater but is transformed quickly into a brilliant showpiece. The male fish develop a pronounced kype, or hooked lower jaw, and their flanks become an intense orange-red with still redder spots showing through. The fins become almost scarlet but still retain the white leading edge common to most chars. Adding to this display, some males develop a black bar extending from nose to tail that creates an almost sinister effect. If any angler is lucky enough to see or catch a male Arctic char in spawning dress, there will be no mistake about what it is. The females show some of this spectacular color but to a lesser degree.

In most of its range an average Arctic char weighs about 5 or 6 pounds. On some rivers in the Northwest Territories the average is a bit larger with some specimens passing the 20-pound mark. Rumors of huge char in some "secret" rivers in northern Quebec weighing over 30 pounds are unconfirmed.

Arctic char are mostly bottom feeders while in freshwater, making them favorites of spinning and baitcasting enthusiasts. They can be caught on flies, however, which are best fished with sinking lines. Flashing silver and gold lures work well on char when they're near river mouths. In totally freshwater, orange, red, and yellow are preferred colors for lures and flies.

GOLDEN TROUT
(*Oncorhynchus aguabonita*)

There are a number of obscure trout species in the western states that are seldom caught or even available to anglers. Among them are the Apache and Gila trout. They are closely related to the dominant rainbow (in many cases, it's difficult to determine a pure strain). The same problem exists with the Golden trout, another candidate for the "most beautiful" crown. It has probably been bred out of existence in some streams because of interbreeding, but enough of them still thrive in high mountain lakes in several western states to warrant mention here.

The Golden trout is a celebration of color. Its olive back dissolves into reddish orange on the sides. There are heavy black spots on the tail and usually on the dorsal fin; also, scattered spots on the gill covers and sides. The cheeks and bellies are goldish-red, and purplish-blue parr marks (they look like thumb prints) are evenly spaced along the lateral line. No other trout in the world is so vividly colored.

A great insect feeder, this little native of the Sierra and Rocky Mountain heights will rise freely to dry flies and sunken lures and flies in very small sizes. A 12-incher is about average with anything larger than 15 (about a pound) being a trophy. Goldens up to 10 pounds have been caught, but one that large would be extremely rare.

SUNAPEE TROUT (*Salvelinus areolus*)

If this list were following a taxonomist's chart, the trout and the char would be listed together. This list follows the order of accessibility to anglers—hence the Sunapee trout is at the tail end. Actually, some scientists are not totally sure the true Sunapee trout is even around these days. It's a char and as such has crossbred with lake trout, blueback trout (another rare species), and probably the common brook trout. Named after Lake Sunapee, in New Hampshire, it's not common even there, with brook trout probably having taken over. Deep-water dwellers except at spawning time, these trout seldom have been caught in recent years. If any reader has caught a Sunapee trout, I'd like to hear from you and see a picture of the fish.

ATLANTIC SALMON
(*Salmo salar*)

Most anglers who have had the opportunity to catch this magnificent fish consider it to be the king of the Salmonidae clan. Heralded for centuries as the fish of kings, its leaping and fighting abilities and outstanding table qualities place this fish in a class of its own. Growing fat on the rich food of the north Atlantic, this salmon enjoys a wide range of "home" rivers extending from Greenland to Maine on the western rim of the Atlantic Ocean. In Europe it's found in Iceland, Norway, The British Isles, Ireland, and somewhat less in Spain and Portugal. Rivers flowing into the Baltic Sea also attract Atlantic salmon.

Range of the Atlantic salmon.

The Atlantic salmon is a trophy fish at any size; an angler's first will be long remembered. By law, fishing for Atlantics is done only with flies in N.A.

Like many of the other salmons and chars, the Atlantic salmon is a fall spawner and unerringly finds its way back to the river of its birth for this ritual. This return trip takes a while; from egg to smolt size (from 6 to 10 inches long) the young salmon remain in their natal stream for two to five years, feeding mostly on insects. At some magic moment in the spring, the young salmon become silvery in coloration and descend the rivers en masse to begin a different life in the ocean. There they grow much faster on a diet of capelin and prawns, and within a year weigh 4 to 5 pounds. Some of these juvenile salmon (grilse) return to the spawning river at that time. Other individuals remain in the ocean for two, three or more years growing still more in length and weight. Salmon with two years of sea-growth average between 10 and 12 pounds and those with three or more can weigh upwards of 20 pounds. Fish with five or six years of uninterrupted ocean feeding are the behemoths of Norway, and in a few rivers in Quebec 50-pound-plus fish are occasionally caught. The average salmon caught in North America weighs about 9 pounds.

In most rivers, identifying the Atlantic salmon is easy because it will be the largest fish caught

As with many large trout today, Atlantic salmon are often released to complete their spawning and perhaps be caught another day.

and perhaps the only fish taken during that particular season. In some European rivers, where sea-run brown trout are common, a problem can exist. Such fish look much like salmon in their silvery mode, and until the fish have been in freshwater for a week or more, separating the two can be difficult. Generally, the salmon has fewer spots, seldom any on the tail. The tail of the salmon is also more deeply curved inward (not really forked) and the maxillary bone (exter-

nal upper jaw) is not as long as the brown trout's. The adipose fin on the brown trout is usually larger than that of the salmon.

Among the tiny fingerlings of 3 to 6 inches that are frequently caught in many salmon rivers in Iceland and Europe, distinguishing salmon from trout can be very difficult. They appear identical at first glance. The salmon parr has a more deeply forked tail and a shorter maxillary bone, which seldom extends past the eye. The brown

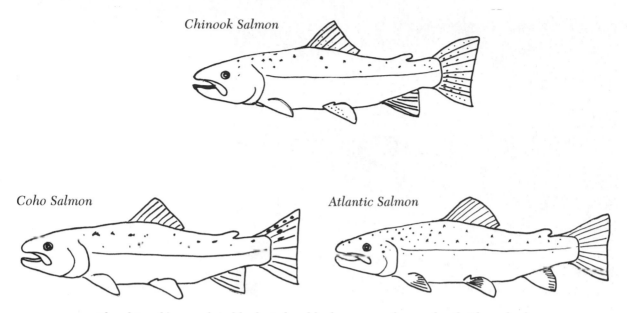

Chinook Salmon

Coho Salmon

Atlantic Salmon

The chinook's mouth is black. It has black spots on fins and tail. The coho has black spots on the upper half of the tail but none on the fins. The Atlantic salmon has black spots on the back and a few on the gill cover, but none on the tail.

trout parr usually displays a reddish adipose fin and several spots on the gill cover. In North America, the other salmonlike fish that the angler will encounter will most likely be brook trout, Arctic char, and an occasional lake trout. None of these have the loose scales of the salmon nor do they have any black spots.

LANDLOCKED SALMON
(*Salmo salar*)

This fish is essentially an Atlantic salmon that does not have access to the sea. During the last Ice Age, some Atlantic salmon were trapped in freshwater and made the best of it. These fish are identical in most ways to Atlantic salmon but can vary considerably in size and color due to available food and water conditions.

The landlocked salmon is one of New England's most popular game fish and is widely distributed in Maine and eastern Canada. A few lakes in New York State offer fishing for them, and they have been highly successful as transplants in Argentina.

Usually known as Ouananiche in Canada, the average landlocked salmon there is a 4-pound fish with some lakes giving up 8- to 10-pounders each year. Landlocked salmon in Maine generally run about a pound or so smaller, with a 3-pounder being close to the norm. They are a great light-tackle fish, jumping and running just like their ocean-going brothers, the Atlantic salmon.

CHINOOK SALMON
(*Oncorhynchus tshawytscha*)

Depending on where the angler finds himself, this fish is variously known as king, tyee, spring, and some unpronounceable Indian names. Whatever it's called, it's a hard-fighting, good-tasting migrant that has been known to reach the 100-pound mark. Forty pounds is considered a big one with 15 pounds being close to average. Entering Pacific rivers from Alaska to California and now heavily stocked in the Great Lakes, the Chinook is one of America's most popular game fish. It is also an important commercial species.

A fresh chinook salmon caught in saltwater near the mouth of a British Columbia river. This 10-pounder is average size, but these salmon grow much larger.

Unlike the Atlantic salmon, which is a totally different species, all salmon which originate in Pacific drainage waters die after spawning. Physically, their bodies simply deteriorate once eggs and sperm are released, whereas Atlantic salmon are capable of spawning again if they can make it back to the sea for a period of rejuvenation.

Range of the Pacific salmon.

The chinook salmon is marked on the back halfway down its sides and on dorsal and tail fins with odd-shaped black spots. A sure means of identification are the black gums inside the lip. Otherwise, it's a typical silvery ocean-going fish that turns very dark with coppery overtones after being in freshwater for a few weeks.

Various races of chinooks enter freshwater at different times. Some leave the sea as early as January and some wait until late summer. Spawning times also vary. This staggered migration appears to be nature's way of assuring continuance of species by providing breeding stock even if there is a natural calamity such as a flood or drought.

COHO SALMON
(*Oncorhynchus kisutch*)

Also known in many regions as silver salmon, the coho is another one of the outstanding Pacific varieties of salmon that battles as good as it tastes. It is primarily a fall spawner and is not as important as a commercial species as are the chinook and some other salmon. This fish has been stocked in the Great Lakes since the mid-60s and, like the chinook, has been a great

A coho salmon from Lake Erie caught while trolling with casting tackle. Pacific salmon were introduced to the Great Lakes twenty-five years ago and have flourished in their new habitat.

success there. Cohos do not grow as large as chinooks, but some fish have been caught in the 30-pound bracket. Eight to 10 pounds is about the national average, in fresh or salt water.

Cohos are quite similar to chinooks when they are in the 5- to 10-pound range. Both fish are bright and silvery when caught in the ocean or in one of the Great Lakes, or when they first enter rivers. The key difference is the color of their gums: the cohos are white. There are fewer spots on the backs and sides of cohos than on chinooks, and there are only a few irregular spots on the upper half of the tail fin. Cheeks and flanks sometimes have a rosy glow not unlike those of an ocean-going rainbow trout. Also like the rainbow, the coho salmon is a strong leaper.

SOCKEYE SALMON
(*Oncorhyncus nerka*)

Not widely popular as a game fish, the sockeye ought to be. It enters many of the same rivers other salmon and steelhead do on the West Coast and when hooked fights long and hard. The sockeye is the most important salmon to the canning industry. Millions are netted each year in estuaries and a few in rivers. Good tasting before they enter freshwater, sockeyes begin to deteriorate soon after leaving the ocean. In fact, it seems like a race with time for spawning salmon to mate before they die—which all Pacific salmon do after breeding.

There are some landlocked sockeyes known as kokanees in a number of far-western lakes and rivers which once had access to the sea. These "baby" sockeyes seldom weigh more than a pound or so but are highly prized as sport and food fish. They are active feeders and can be

Sockeyes will hit all sorts of flies and lures. This one went for a big orange streamer fly in an Alaskan coastal river.

A mean-looking male sockeye salmon in full spawning dress. Large hooked jaws and huge fatty hump on the back with crimson sides positively identify this fish.

caught on flies, small spinning lures, and a wide variety of natural baits. Kokanees, like arctic char, are at their best as food when smoked.

PINK SALMON (*Oncorhynchus gorbuscha*)

Another highly important commercial species, the pink salmon is widely distributed on both sides of the Pacific Ocean, with good populations in northern Japan, Alaska, Canada, and south to California. Long thought to be a rather difficult fish to catch, the pink does hit a variety of spin-

ning lures, flies, and flashing spoons. Body shape is much like that of the other Pacific salmon and so is its general silvery color when fresh from the ocean. While in saltwater and, for a short time, in fresh, the pink salmon does indeed show an overtint of pinkish purple on its flanks. The tail and dorsal fin are heavily spotted with irregular dots and dashes.

There are other species of Pacific salmon, but they are not generally considered important angling targets. Most of them are caught incidentally since they strike the same lures and baits that appeal to the more frequently caught species.

Another fine sport fish is the pink salmon. Not as large as the chinook or coho, the pinky will hit a wide variety of red-and-silver lures. Note the heavily spotted tail and blotch of white on the side—typical pink salmon markings.

GRAYLING
(*Thymallus arcticus*)

Range of the Arctic grayling.

Not a true trout or salmon, the grayling is usually lumped in with them in most angling books because of its troutlike habits. A spring spawner, the beautiful grayling prefers fast moving water for this chore and remains there much of the year. There are a few grayling in Montana and bordering western states, but most fishing for them takes place in Alaska and western Canada.

There's no mistaking a grayling for any other fish. Its high, sail-like dorsal fin is unlike that of any other freshwater species, as is its grayish color. On this metallic background are a few black spots and little else. The dorsal fin, particularly that of the males, is heavily spotted with

Arctic grayling are fond of small lures and flies, and put on a good show when hooked. The high dorsal fin with lavender dots and dashes is unlike that of any other freshwater fish.

lavender dots sometimes edged in purple. The pectoral and ventral fins may also show some lavender in the shape of stripes and dashes. It is an extremely handsome fish.

It's too bad the grayling isn't more widely distributed in the contiguous lower 48 because it is one of the most willing takers of small dry and wet flies. A great fish for the beginning fly fisherman, it jumps like a rainbow trout and fights valiantly for its size. An average grayling in most waters seldom weighs 2 pounds and a trophy about twice that. One of the finest food fish in the world, they taste best when broiled at streamside.

2

Spinning Tackle

One advantage spinning tackle offers the trout angler is its ability to cast small lures and baits a considerable distance. Another advantage, and no less significant, is that, after making the cast, all you have to do is retrieve the line (by turning the reel handle); the spinning lure provides the action. It's an easy and trouble-free way to fish. Many first-time anglers become instant converts when they chose spinning gear as their initial equipment.

The history of precisely where and how modern spinning reels evolved is somewhat clouded. There is strong evidence that wrapping line around a stick or round stone and then tossing the bait or lure by hand, allowing its weight to pull line from this line holder, was practiced by primitive anglers. In principle, this arrangement was an extremely unsophisticated spinning reel. The British were fishing with far more advanced spinning gear nearly a century before such rods and reels came to these shores. Spinning did not become a major angling method until the 1940s. It's fair to say that 50 percent of the trout caught in the world today are taken on spinning tackle.

With that 50 percent figure in mind, it follows that fishing-tackle makers would offer a wide choice of gear. Do they ever! At least 1,000 different rods are collectively cataloged at the moment. Add those offered by custom rod builders and the list grows even longer.

SPINNING REELS

The options available in spinning reels are vast and varied. If one were to set about testing and evaluating every size and model made in the world today, the job would never end. It couldn't because before this year's crop could be examined, umpteen dozen new, "improved" designs would have been introduced. As we've already noted, the fishing-tackle market is highly competitive and the reel makers are constantly trying to get a jump on the other guys. As a result, spinning reels have never been better than they are today—and they'll even be better tomorrow!

The quality of spinning reels and their on-the-water performance is not linked as closely to

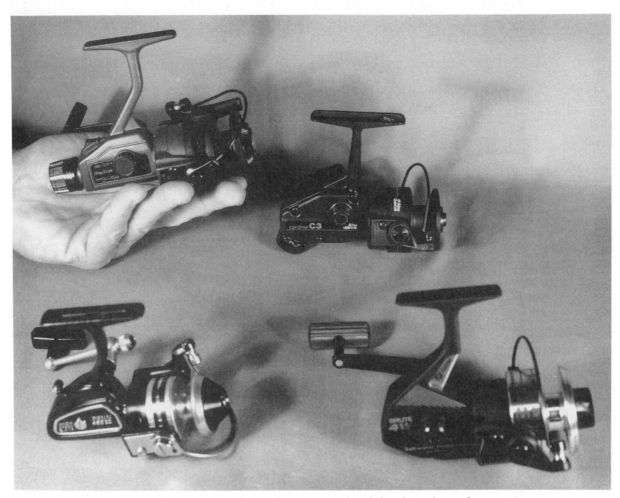

Spinning reels on the market today are mostly of the skirted-spool type. Many reels can be converted for either left- or right-handed anglers.

price as it is with most other tackle items. This is probably due to constant experimenting and modifying by the makers. So—what's the first-time spinning-reel buyer to do? As with a number of other tackle decisions, the best move is to ask an experienced angler which spinning reel he's using at the moment and why. Like automobile owners, anglers are not reticent about voicing their preferences. To be sure, there are some unfounded prejudices that are bound to show up but listen and act accordingly. You won't go far wrong.

I've used spinning reels made by two-dozen makers, at least, and few of them have been real clunkers. Those that failed did so because they either had poor drag systems, were built of inferior synthetics and metals, or were assembled in a shoddy manner. Until you have fished a lot and had the opportunity to test many reels, it's wise to limit your choice to the better-known names in the tackle industry. Their guarantees and repair policies are better, and since they've been around a while they know what they're doing. That's not to say that some fledgling company can't deliver a first-class product. Some of them can and do, but the novice is better served by sticking with the good old brand names.

Berkley, Shakespeare, Penn, Daiwa, Ryobi, Mitchell, Eagle Claw, Shimano, Lew Childre, and Zebco are all well known and trusted spinning-reel makers. The current batch of mail-order houses, most of which offer spinning reels bearing their house name, also offer excellent products and reliable service.

The trout angler who's going to be tossing small to medium-size spinning lures and perhaps a variety of natural baits needs only one reel. It should have the following features:

1. A capacity of 150 yards or more of 6-pound line.
2. A skirted spool that is easily removed.
3. A smooth drag that can be adjusted quickly.
4. A reel handle that cranks smoothly.
5. A solid and gap-free assembly.

Checking the line capacity of most spinning reels is easy. That information is printed on the spools of the majority of them. If it isn't you'll find it on the box or in the accompanying literature. Reels that will accept 150 yards or more of 6-pound line will also handle line testing up to 12 pounds—but less of it.

Skirted spools, those that extend back and over the reel shaft, are standard fare, but make sure the spool is easy to remove. Some reels give up their spools reluctantly. It's a good idea to buy an extra spool in case you want to change line in a hurry.

Intelligent checking of the drag can't really be done without having some line on the reel. Take a few feet with you to the tackle shop. Wind it up on the reel spool and pull it off, first smoothly and then with quick jerks. No need to tighten the drag with a vengeance—you'll never need all the tension you can apply. If the clerk or owner objects to your doing this, try another shop.

General appearance and workmanship are not all that difficult to judge. If a reel just looks and feels solid it probably is. Junk speaks for itself and requires little examination.

As you fish more and develop your own prefer-

Spool capacity for lines of various pound-tests are printed on most modern spinning reels.

ences you may want to buy more reels. But I've found that a spinning reel that can handle 6- to 12-pound line will cover practically all trout fishing coast to coast and world-wide as well. With the exception of deep trolling and large river fishing where extremely long casts are required, it will do just fine for a lot of salmon fishing, too.

SPINCAST REELS

The spincast reel, as the name implies, is a sort of half-and-half combination of spinning and casting reel. It mounts on top of the rod handle like a casting reel, but the line is wound around a spool that does not revolve, like a spinning reel. The line spool is encased in a conical-shaped cover which prevents it from tangling and forces the line to enter the rod guides at a constant angle. A complex explanation for a basically simple device, I'll admit, but it is the easiest of all reels to cast. As a beginner's reel for casting lures or live bait it has no equal.

The vast majority of spincast reels are activated by pressing on a rear-mounted button that disengages the pin holding the line on the spool. As the rod is moved foward the thumb is lifted and the line spins from the spool. Spincast reels, while suitable for perhaps 75 percent of all fresh-

water fishing, have certain limitations. They don't have as much line capacity as do spinning or casting reels and they're more difficult to control when trying for extreme accuracy. Spincast reels received bad press for many years for having poor drag systems, but this is no longer true. Some currently made spincast reels are equipped with excellent drag systems and cast very smoothly.

If you use a spincast reel a lot, you'll want to change line often. The stop-and-start system inherent in these reels is bit tough on monofilament. For this reason, extremely fine-diameter lines don't work well on spincasters. Most manufacturers supply these reels with 10-pound test line on the spools. This is a good choice for them and will work well for all but the most refined trout fishing.

Spincast reels are not as expensive as good-quality spinning or casting reels. This is a consideration for economy-minded buyers, but again, you do get what you pay for. Select one using the same criteria applied to other reels: smoothness of operation, firm, nonrattling action, and good overall workmanship. If you're not sure, stick with a well-known manufacturer: Zebco, Daiwa, Johnson, Mitchell, Shakespeare, Eagle Claw, and Shimano offer excellent spincast reels.

It's worth mentioning that spincast reels are a

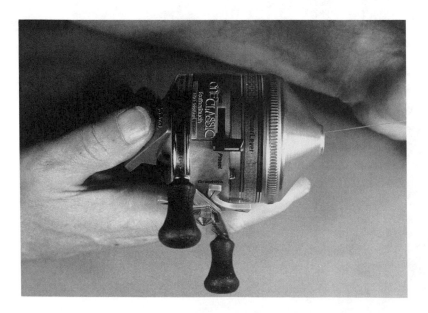

Spincast reel is a perfect choice for many beginners since the line is not touched during casting. Line tangles are rare and the pushbutton operation is nearly foolproof.

big help when casting at night. Make a cast, crank the lure, and cast again. The spincast reel practically eliminates tangles.

SPINNING RODS

A spinning rod for trout fishing should match your reel. A 6-foot, medium-action rod marked for use with 6- to 12-pound-test line is the right choice. It's the right choice because the length won't be in the way on many small streams and it's still long enough to make more distant casts or softly lob a live bait. It's also the rod most experienced spin fishermen choose for 90 percent of their trout angling. Choose a rod with a flexible tip and some reserve power in the butt. Such an action is a product of design. As the rod fibers are wound around the mandrel, or rod-shaping form, the taper and wall thickness are created. By increasing or decreasing the degree of taper and adding or subtracting material, the final action is built-in. This is the way all graphite and graphite/glass composite rods are made. It's far more complicated than this brief explanation offers—a hundredth of an inch can make a tremendous difference in rod performance.

Fortunately, we don't have to worry much about how rods are made, but only how well they do their intended jobs.

A lot of talk on the stream and in the monthly periodicals revolves around "ultra-light" spinning. To most anglers this term means fishing with a very short, lightweight rod and a tiny reel loaded with 2- or 4-pound line. Very large trout can be landed on such tackle and casts to seemingly impossible spots can be made—if the spots aren't too far away. However, fishing with such tackle is an expert's game and even the experts don't use it all the time. Making long casts with rods shorter than 5 feet is difficult and so is applying enough pressure on sizable fish. Using diminutive tackle is, however, a lot of fun with pan-size fish. Try the short rod and 2-pound line if you wish, but be prepared for some frustrations.

The 6-foot spinning rod suggested ought to feature most of the exterior qualities recom-

For lure fishing in rivers where a lot of casting is required, spinning tackle is the first choice of anglers today.

mended for the casting rod: A neat appearance, nice looking hardware, and five or more guides. A locking reel seat is preferred (a threaded collar that holds the reel firmly) as is a comfortable grip that's long enough to use both hands for casting if you choose.

Within this general description, a buyer can find a dozen rods or more in most tackle stores. A few glass rods at very low prices are available and if one feels okay and appears to be well made it will probably do the job.

Far more rods today are built from graphite and graphite/glass composites, making the options much broader. It is the best choice for that reason and several more. Graphite snaps back to a straight attitude much quicker after it's bent than does glass. When casting, this means that as the rod is flexed and line is released, the lure being cast does so with greater velocity. In short, you can cast farther with graphite than you can with glass. Graphite is also about two-thirds the weight of glass, a factor which can be highly important at the end of a long fishing day.

Experienced anglers like graphite for a special reason: It is an extremely sensitive material that transmits the slightest tremor from the unseen end of the line. When baitfishing or deep jigging, such a sense of "feel" is of great help if the fish are striking softly. Sometimes even the largest trout can grab a lure or bait quite tenderly.

This basic spinning rod will do a fine job with most live baits if a "soft" cast is used to avoid losing the bait when it's released. Worms, some minnows, crayfish, salmon eggs, and other soft things and creatures are highly prone to go flying off in some other direction during a regular overhead cast. A soft cast is made side-arm, the line released while the rod is still moving, as opposed to releasing with a *snap* as you would with a lure. Twenty minutes of practice on grass will reveal the style.

The very best rod for casting live bait with a spinning reel is a "noodling" rod. Before long, limber rods were built with spinning guides at-

A long, flexible spinning rod is ideal for river fishing. Such a rod will protect light line when a large fish strikes by bending to absorb the impact.

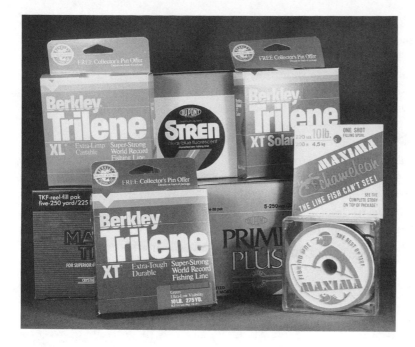

Monofilament line is standard for all spinning reels. This is the link between you and your fish, so buy a well-known brand.

tached, anglers who wanted to use this approach simply taped a spinning reel to a fly rod. It worked reasonably well, but a rod properly designed for the spinning reel is much more satisfactory. These long, sensitive rods are ideal for drifting a nightcrawler, salmon egg, or other fragile bait along a rocky bottom. Six-pound-test line is perfect for most trout fishing and eight- or ten-pound material is heavy enough for most steelhead trout and salmon. The long rod acts as a shock absorber in protecting the lighter line.

MONOFILAMENT LINE

For nearly half a century, monofilament line has been the standard connecting strand between man and fish. It is the kind of line most often spooled on spinning, casting, and trolling reels. Monofilament is also the material used for fly leaders. I can think of no other product that so completely dominates an outdoor activity the way monofilament controls the sport of fishing.

Of course, fishing was a popular activity before nylon monofilament was invented in the late 1930s, but it was not done with the efficiency provided by this wonder product. Braided cot-

ton, linen, and silk lines were once the standards, with silkworm "gut" and tail hairs from horses being the best available materials for fly leaders.

The early formulas of "mono" were not, to be charitable, all that reliable. They were not of uniform diameter, were much too stiff for decent casting, and lost a great deal of strength when knots were tied. But linemakers, being good business people, realized that mono line could become the "razor blade" commodity of fishing. You use it until it's worn and then buy some more. Sales potential was great. The research and development applied to monofilament line has been intense and continues to be. It's reached a point where it's difficult to understand how modern monos can be improved, yet new versions are introduced almost annually that are claimed to be better.

Not being a chemist, I don't fully understand how "pellets" of solid nylon are formed. These solid pellets are dumped into a hopper and melted; the liquid is then forced through a tiny hole; and presto, out comes monofilament fishing line. Those who make mono line are probably rolling on the floor with laughter or agony at reading that simple explanation. But that's really the way it works, and all an angler has to know about the manufacturing process. What he should know more about is which monofilament to buy and how to use it.

Unless you're on the most limited budget in the world, the only brands of monofilament one should consider buying are those from the better-known companies. There is a lot of "brand-X" mono around, and while it may be okay, a heap of it is, well, indifferent. The well-publicized makers can't afford to attach their names to shoddy material. Their products must live up to expectations as well as be true to the information printed on the label. Among these better-known labels, it's safe to say, the monofilament line is excellent. But, it is different.

Limp and Stiff Mono

Some monofilaments are quite limp whereas others are more rigid, or "stiff." Between these extremes, lie most of the monos we fish with. Stiff monos are said to have more "memory" than limp ones since they tend to want to remain coiled once they've been on a reel for a few weeks. While line that is too stiff and kinky is an abomination to cast, it works well as leader material or for trolling once it's straightened out. Limp line casts better from revolving spool (casting) reels. Mono with a bit of stiffness works best on spinning reels. Manufacturers in general try to incorporate a blend of both into their products in order to offer a compromise.

The big names in the mono business, Dupont and Berkeley, list several versions of mono. There are some key words on their labels that offer clues to which is stiffer or limper, but these words change from time to time. The best advice is to purchase the one featured by your tackle store for starters. If it casts well on your reel, fine. If not, the next time buy a different formula or brand.

A quick look at the rack of monofilament line in the tackle store will reveal spools holding varying amounts. The literature in your reel box or the numbers printed on the reel will indicate how much to buy. It's more than annoying to run out of line before the reel spool is full, so be sure to buy enough. In fact, if you expect to be fishing

a great deal it's not a bad idea to buy an extra spool. Always buy extra if you're going on an extended trip or to some location beyond the shopping malls.

Test and Color

Four, 6- and 8-pound-test monofilament are the most useful for small and medium-size trout, meaning those up to about 16 or 18 inches. In larger rivers or lakes or where fish of 2 feet or more may be expected, 10- and 12-pound-tests are not out of place. If you're casting lures weighing a half ounce or more, 8 pound is about as light as one can use without some breaking problems.

With very small lures (and small fish), line as light as 2 pounds can be useful but care must be taken when playing fish or getting snagged on the bottom. Reel drag must be smooth in order to handle a sizable fish on 2-pound line.

Lines for trolling are generally subject to more abuse and should be correspondingly stronger. This is particularly the case when trolling with downriggers. Snapping the line in and out of downrigger clips takes its toll, and the line must be examined frequently for nicks and abrasions. If you feel a rough section or see an obviously frayed spot, cut the line back and retie the lure.

Among the monofilament lines available, a wide variety of colors and shades of colors will be noted along with degrees of "shine," or florescence. Florescent substances are added to some line formulas when they are blended. This shiny gleam helps the angler see his line and, in some cases, can be a great advantage. When several lines are being trolled from the same boat being able to identify which line is coming from which rod can avoid some terrible tangles. There is a major difference of opinion, however, among experienced anglers when it comes to the fish-catching differences between florescent and nonflorescent monofilaments.

There are many highly skilled anglers and professional guides with vast experience on fresh and saltwater who wouldn't be caught with florescent mono on their reels. There are others who use it but insist on attaching a section of nonflorescent material to the end of their line. They don't want the shiny stuff next to the lure or bait. A third group insists that the fish don't care and can't distinguish between the florescent and the plain material.

Since the fish aren't talking and aren't likely to, we'll probably never know the correct answer. I'm a middle-of-the-roader when it comes to spinning, casting, and trolling. I use florescent materials for trolling and deep jigging because it is easy to see, but I also tie on a 4- to 6-foot leader of clear material—just in case. This leader is always a few pounds heavier than the line itself. With 6-pound mono for example, a leader testing twice that is about right. With 12-pound, 15 or 17 clear mono is a good choice. The heavier material next to the lure is insurance against tooth abrasion, hang-ups, and other mishaps. The thicker line also lasts longer if much lure changing is done. When it looks a bit "used up," tie on another piece. Serious abrasions can be seen and nicks and cuts be felt by sliding a fingernail along the suspected section.

For most casting and spinning in lakes and streams I stick with clear or tinted monofilament with no florescence. In these situations the lure or hook is tied directly to the mono with no leader considered. No, I can't prove it makes a difference but I *think* is does and that gives me reason to fish with a little more confidence (hey, no one ever said that anglers were logical!).

For fly leaders for trout or salmon, fluorescent material is not considered. Too many last second refusals by spooky trout and salmon have convinced me that the shiny material next to flies is a no-no. I prefer slightly tinted or clear material for this work and if tinted, olive or pale brown is the choice.

Other than being limp or stiff, there are several other properties built into monofilament line. Knot strength, abrasion resistance, stretch, water-absorption factor, and tensile strength. All of these properties can be controlled by the chemists to a point. When one property is increased too much, another is affected. For example: knot strength could be increased at the risk of increasing stretch, which could adversely affect hooking ability. Therefore, the ideal mono is one that combines all properties into the best compromise.

Tensile strength or pound-test simply means how much weight can be hung on the line before it breaks. This is the property most anglers are concerned with. We all fret about how strong our line is. The worry is not as great as it might be because the manufacturers tell a "little white lie" here. Unless otherwise marked, all monofilament line actually tests a pound or more than the number shown on the label. Some 6-pound-test mono will withstand over 10 pounds of dead weight before breaking. This is not cheating on the part of the makers. They are obliged to produce a line that will not break *below* the stated figure so they solve it by adding a cushion of a pound or so. This serves most anglers well, but it must be remembered that if you enter a trophy fish in a well-regulated competition you could be in for a surprise. If the maximum line test in a specific category calls for 6-pound, and your "6"-pound line proves to be stronger, your entry will be disqualified. If you choose to fish for "the record" buy a line that breaks *under* the line category you intend to enter. These premium monofilaments are supplied by the better manufacturers and are so marked.

Putting Line on the Reel

When spooling monofilament line on a reel, spool it on in *the direction that it leaves the spool*. Otherwise, you could be in for some tangled casting due to the built-in "set" in the line. If the line remains kinky and difficult to manage, allow it to trail behind a moving boat until the curls are straightened out and then rewind it snugly.

The manufacturers will love me for saying it, but it's true that monofilament line should be replaced often if it's received a lot of use. Cutting off the first few feet whenever it looks a bit frayed is the right thing to do. When enough short sections have been removed, it's time to buy some more. It's false economy to just "get by" on worn line or not enough of it. The fish of your dreams is bound to strike when you're not properly prepared. The reel should be filled to about 1/16 inch from the lip of the spool.

HOW TO CAST: SPINNING

There are two basic casts with a spinning outfit—the overhead and the side cast. Unless there are overhanging trees, you can cast farther and more accurately with the overhead cast, illustrated below.

1

Grip the rod with the reel leg between the second and third fingers, thumb on top. Rotate the reel's cowling until the line roller is directly under your extended index finger. Pick up the line with the fleshy tip of the index finger and open the bail. The lure should suspend about 12 inches below the tip.

2

Point the rod tip at the target at about the 10 o'clock position. Your wrist should be aligned with the rod handle and your elbow close to your side.

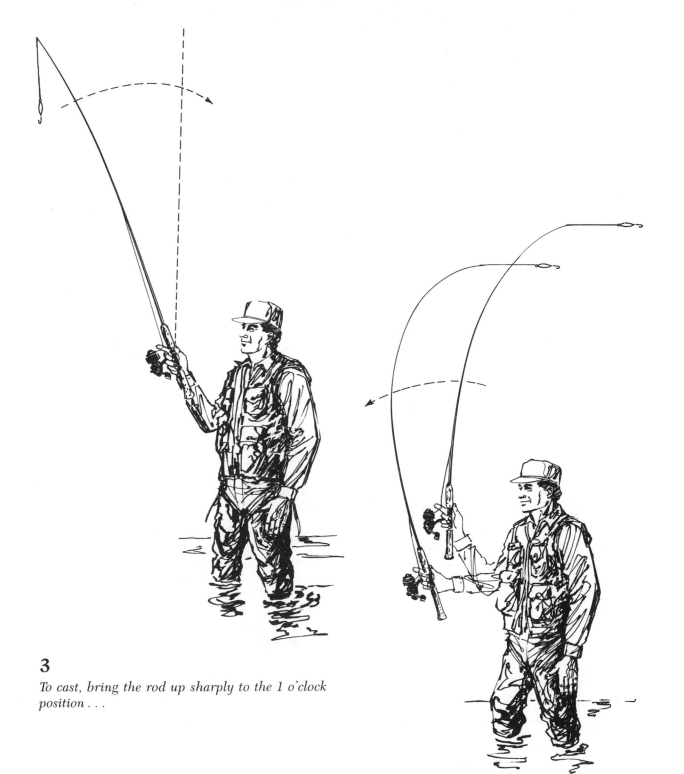

3

To cast, bring the rod up sharply to the 1 o'clock position . . .

4

. . . and allow the weight of the lure to flex the rod to the rear. At maximum flex, snap the rod forward . . .

 STEP 5 →

5

. . . to the 11 o'clock position and extend the index finger, releasing the line and sending the lure toward the target. As the lure nears the target, apply gentle pressure to the line with the tip of your index finger. When the lure hits the water, press the finger against the edge of the spool, stopping the line from uncoiling further.

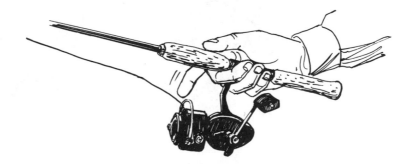

SPINCASTING

Casting with a top-mounted spincast reel is basically the same as casting with an open-face spinning reel, with these exceptions.

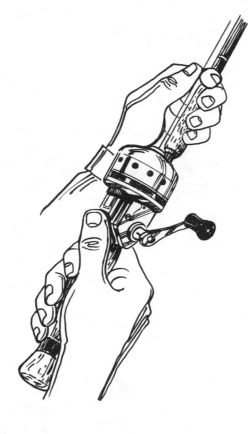

1

For maximum accuracy, grip the rod as shown, the right hand below the reel, thumb on release button, the left hand above the reel, holding the rod between the first two fingers, the line between the thumb and index finger. The lure should hang about 12 inches below the rod tip. Perform the overhead cast as with a spinning reel, but with both hands on the rod, and release the thumb button and the line at 11 o'clock to send the lure toward the target.

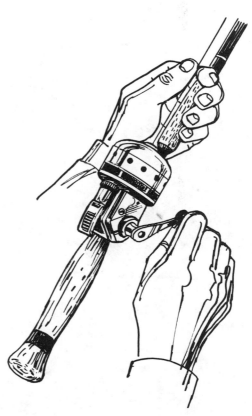

2

To retrieve line, retain grip above the reel with the left hand and crank line with the right. Apply slight tension on the line. This cleans the line and aids in winding it tightly onto the spool.

3

Fly Tackle

RODS

Fly rods are made to perform a highly specialized function. Unlike spinning and casting rods, they must be able to support a rather heavy fly line as it is *false cast* in the air. In fly casting it's *the weight of the line* that carries the leader, with fly attached, to the intended target. In spinning and casting it's the weight of the lure pulling line from the reel that accomplishes that task.

Every fly rod is designed to throw a line of a specific weight. The weights have been standardized and given numbers, so that no matter what brand you buy, you'll get a line of the same weight.

Fly rods are rated for lines from size 2 to 13. We'll discuss lines later in this chapter, but for now, consider this rule of thumb: if the trout (or salmon) in the waters you fish most range from 6 inches to 6 pounds, then a 6-weight outfit is perfect. (Let me assure you, a 6-pound trout is a trophy at most trout stream parking lots.) The same guideline holds for line sizes 2 through 7. From size 8 and up, the rule doesn't totally apply

because here we're getting into fly-rod gear for much larger fish. More about that in the salmon chapters.

An 8- or 8½-foot fly rod handling a 6-weight line is the ideal outfit for a beginner. There's a huge choice of fly rods in this range. Every company that makes fly rods lists one, and if they don't they're not paying attention. To their great credit, rod makers don't produce many "dogs" today. A few fly-by-night marketers make some junk, but they don't last long, and reputable tackle shops won't bother stocking them. It's easy to spot the unsatisfactory rods. They have too few guides, too much plastic, and are usually painted a garish color.

While a few excellent glass rods may still be found, graphite and graphite/composite fly rods make up the lion's share of quality products. These shafts are light, resilient, durable, and sensitive.

Our basic fly rod should fish well at moderate distances as well as up close and at longer ranges. The rod should be able to toss small or large flies. It should not overpower small trout and yet have

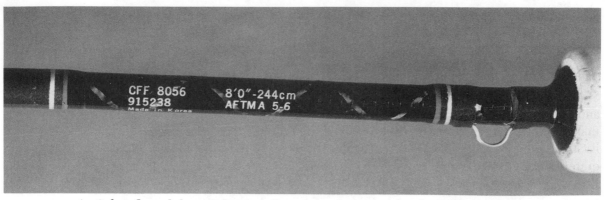

An 8-foot fly rod designed to handle a 6-weight line is the ideal choice for the novice trout angler.

some reserve strength to handle that dream fish should we be lucky enough to hook it. A large order? Lucky for us, such rods are in tackle shops by the dozen. The rub is, it's not easy to pick one up, give it a wiggle or two, and know if it's the right one for you.

That *ideal* fly rod should have a sensitive tip that will protect fine leaders and still not be "wimpy" in the butt section. When a rod like this is bent from the pull of a fish or flexed when casting, it should display a progressive arc. Put another way, it should bend in a parabolic curve instead of a half circle. Some excellent rods do bend in a near perfect arc, and a lot of anglers cast well with them. This is one of the mysteries of fly casting. Each of us has a highly personal set of reflexes because our muscles and hand-eye coordination are different. That's why some football players throw the ball, some catch it, and others do the tackling and kicking. Rods that work "quickly," that snap back to a straight attitude in a hurry, require faster reflexes to cast well. Rods that are slower, or take more time to complete the bend-and-straighten cycle, are best used by those of us who aren't as speedy as others. In spite of sounding complicated, casting enough fly line on the water to catch trout is really quite easy. If you can walk and chew gum at the same time, you'll have little difficulty.

The greatest number of fly rods are of the two-piece variety. They come apart at the center connection (the ferrule). This ferrule can be a

Rod actions vary considerably and only casting will determine which rod suits you best. If possible, enlist the help of an experienced fly-rodder to assist you in choosing a rod.

sleeve arrangement, with one section sliding over the other, or a plug design in which a solid cylinder is glued fast to one section and inserts into the other. Both systems are well proven and work fine when they are properly fitted. Tip:

glass and graphite ferrules go together and come apart much easier if rubbed with paraffin or candle wax.

Fly rods of that ideal configuration we've been discussing can be found at a wide range of prices. Some economy glass rods, complete with reel and line and offered as "kits," are sold by several makers. Martin and Shakespeare, for example, list kits selling for less than $35.00 and they're quite serviceable. Kits from Cortland and Berkley are slightly higher in price, and those from the well-known mail-order houses such as Orvis, Thomas and Thomas, and Cabela's go into the hundreds of dollars.

Fly rods are made by at least fifty companies, and most of them have their virtues and their fans. Every angler eventually discovers the rod that pleases him or her most, and it's impossible to say positively that this or that one is *better*. Some excellent graphite fly rods are available today that retail for about $50. Some of them perform as well or better than others costing twice as much. Rods in the $100 to $150 range are as fishable as anything made in the world. Above that price, you're paying for extra-fine finish, top-quality hardware, and reputation. Of course, you're also buying some intangibles like pride of ownership, and a bit of magic that only fly-rodders come to understand.

Coming on strong in the fly rod scene are multi-piece rods which break down to four or more sections. Several of these are being offered by the most famous names in fly tackle and by a few newcomers. Loomis, Fisher, Orvis, Thomas

Standard grip on most fly rods is made of cork and comes in different shapes. Choose one that fits your hand. This is the proper way to carry a fly rod, with the butt forward so you won't damage the tip.

and Thomas, Sage, Deerfield, and several others catalog such rods and more probably will. The arrival of graphite rod blanks helped make this possible. Graphite's light weight and great strength enable rod makers to add extra ferrules without adding extra bulk. Travel rods constructed from glass fibers alone once tended to be heavy and not very good casters. They were either too stiff or too limber. Today's multi-piece rods are fully the equal in action of two piece rods and are blessings for the angler who travels a great deal on airlines. The short rod case can be carried under the arm instead of being entrusted to baggage handlers. It's nice to have your rods arrive with you!

My preference for rod handle material is the traditional cork grip. It's durable, reasonably water resistant, and won't twist in the hand. The handle should also have a locking reel seat. There should be at least ten guides, plus the tip-top.

When buying your first rod, it's a good idea to ask a fly fishing pal to accompany you to the tackle store. If possible, assemble the rod and try a few practice casts or have your pal do it. It's not unlike a test drive in an auto you intend to buy. After all, you'll be spending a lot of time with that rod in your hand, we hope, so you may as well feel comfortable with it.

When buying any tackle items, if you're in doubt about precisely what you need, it's best to do your shopping at a store that specializes in fishing gear. It's a good bet that the owner of the store and his employees will be well informed about their merchandise. This is important for all buyers but especially for the novice. If you're absolutely sure about your next tackle purchase, go to the place offering the best price. If not, the "mom and pop" tackle shops can provide a lot of advice and service. They are serious about developing new customers and know that supplying them with the right stuff will bring them back.

FLY REELS FOR TROUT

The fly reel is the most basic reel in the world. It's nothing more than a wheel on an axle sur-rounded by a frame. As the wheel turns on the axle, one way or the other, the line pays out or is retrieved. Yet, this example of primitive simplicity has received more attention over a longer period of time than any other item of tackle. This is even more curious when we consider the fly reel has been thought of as a relatively unimportant piece of tackle by many angler-writers. In a number of books and stories during the first half of this century, the fly reel was often described as being, "only a place to store the line."

I think the reason for this attitude on the part of American writers and anglers was that the fly reel was thought of as being suitable only for small fish, mostly trout measuring 12 inches or so. We did not have the excellent rods, fly lines, and other equipment which today allow us to seek really big fish with fly fishing gear. It can be now said with reasonable certainty that for all types of fishing a good quality reel with a smooth and reliable drag system is the heart of an angling outfit.

If the choice available in rods is staggering, the fly reels on today's market may cause total confusion. With a price spread from under $15 to over $1,000, and all of these a variation of that same "little wheel with a handle on it," non-anglers may have some reason to question our sanity. But it's not unlike choosing a car, boat, house, or fine firearm. We can move from place to place in any sort of vehicle or watercraft. Some of them move faster, some more comfortably—but they all get there. A *nice* house is nothing more than a better cabin, and quail grassed with a $5,000 shotgun taste no better than those gathered with one costing 50 bucks. Beauty and function (a happy combination of all quality fishing tackle) are what most fly fishers eventually seek to hang on their fly rods. What a choice!

In order to find a reasonable starting point as well as a benchmark most trout anglers can live with for a long time, a fly reel that will hold 50 yards of backing (braided line) plus a 6-weight fly line is the best choice. With a reel so equipped, the fly angler can head for 95 percent of all trout streams in the world and feel confident of having the right stuff.

Nearly every company that markets fly reels

offers one that's sized right for a 6-weight line. Because prices at retail stores vary widely, it's impossible to state precisely what numbers you'll find today or tomorrow. For this reason let's use the words, economy, mid-range, high-quality, and top-drawer. Economy means if you can afford to fish at all you can probably swing it. Top-drawer means you don't really need this one but wouldn't it be nice?

Economy

Berkley, Eagle Claw, and Fenwick offer graphite reels in this range that are made for 6-weight lines. They are excellent values and feature "rim-control," which allows the angler to fine-tune drag adjustment when playing a fish. Some inexpensive graphite reels also have internal drag systems that are surprisingly smooth. Berkley's is better than it should be on such an inexpensive reel. These reels are lightweight and have few metal parts that may rust.

All or mostly metal reels in the economy range that represent good values are made by Cort-

land, Shakespeare, South Bend, Pflueger, Martin, Ryobi, L.L. Bean, Orvis, and perhaps another dozen makers. These are mainly of cast or stamped aluminum or some other alloy, with a few, such as the Pflueger Medalist, being of steel.

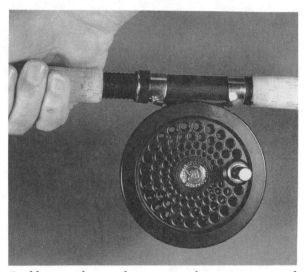

Berkley graphite reels are rugged, nonrusting, and inexpensive—an excellent choice for the beginner.

For over fifty years, the fly reel others are compared to has been the Pflueger Medalist. This moderately priced reel is an American standard and should remain so for a long time.

Scientific Anglers offers a fine selection of reels in their System 2 line. The 2L is a good lightweight reel for fishing small streams.

A few words of praise are due the well-tested Pflueger Medalist. It has long been regarded by many anglers to be an American standard. It is offered in several sizes, but the old Pflueger 1494 remains one of the most often seen reels on trout streams. I wouldn't hesitate to buy a decent second-hand one.

The Martin company deserves kind words too for the wide variety of economy-priced reels (along with some near mid-range models) they are famous for. They are excellent values and more rugged than some high-quality reels.

Mid-Range

A standout in the mid-range group is Scientific Anglers System Two L. It's light, has great capacity, and an adjustable drag that functions well. The Double L model from L.L. Bean and a couple of models from Orvis are also in this group. All are excellent reels. (Later in this book we'll discuss reels and rods for salmon, and there are several other reels in this category that are suitable for them.) For a wider variety of trout reels it's necessary to advance to the next level.

High Quality

This group includes the reels that experienced anglers choose for their fly fishing. Most of them offer nice looks, good drag systems, and solid construction. Among the choices are: The CFOs and Presentation series from Orvis, Fenwick's World Class models, Bean's STH, the Marryat, the Lightweights and Marquis series from Hardy, J. W. Young, CRI, Bill Ballan, API, Sage, Ross, Loomis and several more than I've not examined or may have overlooked.

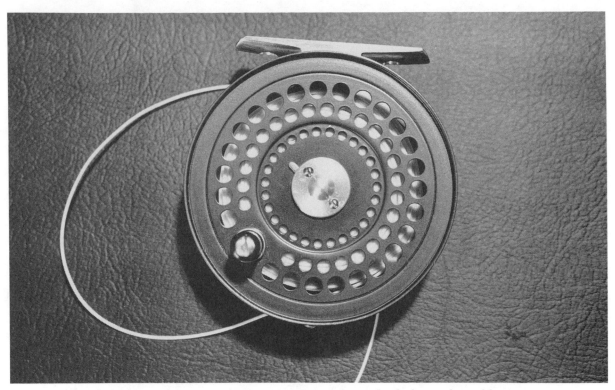

Top choice from Orvis is the CFO in various sizes. This lightweight reel has an amazingly large capacity.

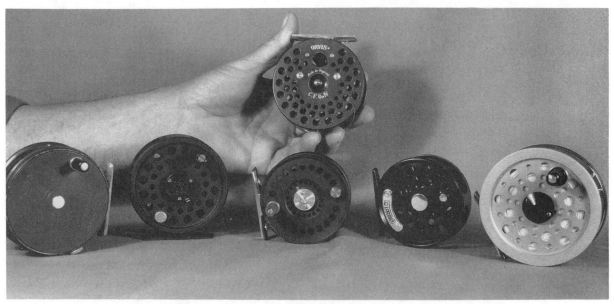

A selection of high-quality reels (from left): Hardy, Thomas and Thomas, Martin, Loomis, Cortland, and, in the hand, Orvis.

Top Drawer

Almost every angler who's had a Stanley Bogdan reel in his hand has nothing but words of praise for it. Bogdan fly reels have become the benchmark top-drawer fly reels. Pre-owned Bogdans command stratospheric prices, and you'll wait three years if you order a new one. They are made one at a time, piece by piece. In case you're interested, write Stanley Bogdan, Nashua, New Hampshire.

An alternative to Bogdan are the semi-production fly reels from Abel. These California beauties are cut from solid aluminum bar stock and feature the smoothest drag system available on any reel currently made. At the moment, they are priced hundreds less than a Bogdan and, considering the extra handwork involved in assembly, are amazing values. The No. 0 or 1 sizes are the ones for trout. In my opinion, they are the finest reels made today.

Other reels falling in this class are literally custom made and are difficult to find and afford. Some anglers seeking the unusual and expensive buy "collector" class reels such as Zwargs, Vom Hofes, antique Hardys, and Leonards for hundreds and thousands of dollars. If reels like this fall into your area of interest, Martin J. Keane, at PO Box 888, Stockbridge, MA 01262, is one of the nation's best known dealers in such merchandise.

FLY LINES

The mechanics of casting a fly line, with fly and leader attached, can be likened to a bumblebee flying; it doesn't seem possible but it works. The

If price is no problem, consider a hand-crafted Bogdan (in hand) or the sleek black Abels. Some consider the Abel to be the best reel in the world.

bumblebee has no idea how it manages to move its tiny wings to propel that fat body through the air—it just does it. The angler moves the long fly rod back and forth and the thick fly line, somehow, unfurls to send the much thinner leader tipped with an air-resistant fly to the desired location. Like the flight of the bumblebee, this seems a mechanical impossibility, but please accept my word that it's much easier than it sounds. It works because of the thick fly line.

Fly casting is impossible without a proper fly line. It cannot be managed with braided or monofilament line alone. The fly line, being the heart of the fly casting outfit, is the one item of tackle that brings it all together. Modern fly lines are marvels of production. Practically all of them are mass produced by machines that lay a coating of PVC (polyvinylchloride) over a braided core of nylon fibers. This coating can be applied in one continuous thickness, resulting in a *level* fly line, or, applied in varying thicknesses, producing *double-tapered* or *weight-forward* lines. The level line is just that, level or of the same diameter throughout its length. The double-tapered line (DT) is thick in the middle and thin on both ends, and the weight forward line (WF) is thin on

How different types of fly lines are tapered.

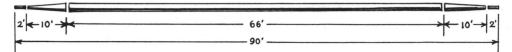

Double Taper. *For casting trout flies and small popping bugs where extreme distance is not required. The larger body section provides weight for casting; the tapered ends assure a light presentation. Line can be reversed for longer use.*

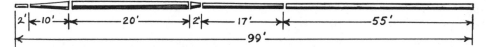

Weight Forward. *For casting large, bushy flies, large streamers, and popping bugs. This line begins like the double taper, with 12 feet of tapered line. But instead of a long level section, there is a 30-foot section of heavy level line, then a quick taper down to a thinner running line for the rest of its length.*

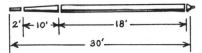

Shooting Taper. *For long-distance casting. Behind the 12-foot taper, there's 18-foot length of heavy level line with a factory-installed loop at the end to which a monofilament or floating line is attached.*

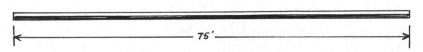

Level Line. *For fishing live bait or situations where long casts or delicate presentation are not required.*

one end, then thick for a few feet and then back to thin again. There are practical reasons for all of these configurations, and all fly line manufacturers comply with the standard sizing system. Numbers indicate the heft of the line and these refer to how many grains each line size weighs. Check the illustration and this becomes clear.

For short casts and baitfishing with a fly rod, a level line will suffice. For more delicate presentation and casts of up to 60 feet, a DT line is preferred. For longer casts and when fishing under windy conditions the WF line is a distinct advantage.

With that *ideal* fly rod discussed earlier, the double-taper floating line (DTF) is the best choice for 90 percent of all trout fishing. They're about three times more expensive than level lines, but they can also be reversed after a season's use and the other unused end can be put into service. If you are frequently casting beyond 60 feet, a weight-forward floating line (WFF) should be considered.

In addition to the floating fly lines, the top fly line manufacturers also offer sinking, sink-tip, and intermediate styles. Sinking fly lines do exactly that and some do it faster or slower. Sinking lines are available in different "sink-rates" and the boxes are so marked. The leading ten feet of most sink-tip fly lines is the sinking part while the rest of the line floats.

Most fly-rod angling can be managed with a floating line, but to fish deep with streamer flies, nymphs, or large wet flies a sinking line is preferred. Casting for steelheads and salmon in larger rivers is a perfect example. Many experienced anglers carry extra reel spools in their vests at all times. When the need to switch from floating line to sinking line arises, it's easy to do so.

Fly lines come in a wide assortment of hues, and it probably doesn't matter which color you select. Since there will be a 6-foot or longer monofilament leader between the thick fly line and the fly, the trout won't care. Choose one you like or one that complements your rod and reel in color photographs. Don't worry about the lengths of the fly lines, either. Most fly lines are between 90 and 100 feet—few anglers can cast that much line.

Which brand of fly line to buy is another of those subjective angling issues. Many good fly lines are made, and while all are quite "fishable" some handle differently. Exterior coatings on fly lines vary. Some are quite hard and a bit on the stiff side, whereas others have a softer, silkier texture. The Cortland 444SL series, for example, has a hard coating and will slide rapidly through the rod guides. This feature makes the 444SL an excellent line for distance casting. The regular 444 lines and the less expensive 333 series feel softer between the fingers and are ideal if a lot of line handling is called for. Casting to a spot here and then there, changing line lengths often, is better done with a soft line.

Scientific Anglers excellent lines are also available with different coating textures. SA's Air Cel Ultra 2 line is a fine compromise of hard and soft finish. It's said to be "self-lubricating," and most anglers who have tried it agree that it is an easy-casting line.

Another fairly hard-finish line that casts nicely is the Specialist from Berkeley. This company features a fly line coating containing "microspheres," which are little air pockets. These tiny chambers are there to help float the line and they do make this one ride like a cork.

Another new group of lines on the market is from Fishtec. They slide through the guides well and appear to be well made. Lee Wulff, one of the genuine legends in the world of fly fishing, markets his own lines labeled "Triangle Taper." They are rated as combination lines and marked 4/5, 6/7, and 8/9. This indicates that they're designed to cover a wide range of rods—and they do it well.

There are several other excellent fly lines available, including those from Orvis, L.L. Bean, and others. They are all satisfactory, and the only way one can determine which is better for his or her style of casting is to try them. This is a solid reason for doing your initial shopping at a store that specializes in fly fishing equipment. At most of these shops you'll be given the opportunity to try a few practice casts and be offered tips on casting. It's worth the effort to seek out this kind of store until you're sure of the rod and line that suits you.

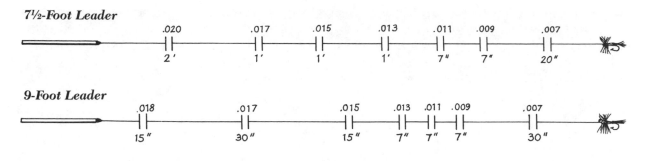

7½-Foot Leader

.020 .017 .015 .013 .011 .009 .007

2' 1' 1' 1' 7" 7" 20"

9-Foot Leader

.018 .017 .015 .013 .011 .009 .007

15" 30" 15" 7" 7" 7" 30"

Braided Line

Because monofilament line functions so well for so many reasons, braided line is not used much today, although it's still excellent for some purposes. As "backing," the auxiliary line on fly reels, nothing else works as well. Since few anglers can cast over 90 feet, that's the length of most fly lines. Large fish may run much farther than that when hooked, so we need more line. Braided Dacron is the preferred material for this purpose. Most anglers use 20-pound test on trout-size reels; 30-pound is better suited for salmon fly-rodding (Check the section on knots to learn how to attach backing to the fly line.)

LEADERS

I suppose the reason a length of monofilament is called a leader is because it "leads" the fly, lure, or bait through the water. The mono leader's primary purpose is to reduce visibility. We're trying to fool the fish into believing that our offering is just there, all by itself.

For fly fishing, we must use a leader whose end is smaller in diameter than the fly line in order to tie on a fly. The thick fly line simply won't pass through the eye of a small hook. Fly leaders are almost always tapered—they are thick at the end attached to the fly line and much thinner at the other end where the fly is tied on. Ready-made fly leaders are available at all stores and mail-order houses that cater to fly anglers. In time, most anglers will want to tie their own using monofilaments of various diameters. The for-

mulas for two basic fly leaders are shown in an accompanying diagram. With slight modifications these leaders are suitable for most trout and salmon fishing.

Leaders for fly fishing are graded according to length and the pound test of their tippets. A 9-foot 4X leader, for example, has a tippet .007 inch in diameter that tests about 3 pounds. Leaders generally are available in lengths from 3 feet up to 15 feet and from 0X (6½ pound test) to 8X (¾-pound test).

Tippet size should be determined by the size of the flies you intend to use. The goal is to present the fly properly and have it appear as natural as possible. It's not necessary, however, to change tippets with each hook size. An 8X or 6X tippet will handle flies in sizes 16 through 24. A 5X, 4X, or 3X tippet is about right for fly sizes 16 through 12; and a 2X, 1X, or 0X will cast flies in sizes 10 through 6.

Store-bought tapered leaders come with a loop at the heavy end. The best way to attach a leader to your fly line is with a loop-to-loop arrangement. To do this, tie an 8-inch length of heavy (.021 inch) mono to the end of the line with a nail knot (see Chapter 12). Then tie a surgeon's loop in the end of the mono. Now you can loop and unloop leaders to your fly line easily.

For very small trout, the plastic line/leader attachment devices will do in a pinch, as will the little metal eyelets that are thrust into the end of the fly line. The eyelets have barbs on one end which hold them in place. Neither of these arrangements work well in practice and can be counted on to fail when you hook the biggest fish of the year.

4

Casting and Trolling Tackle

REELS

To the novice angler the term "baitcasting" is a bit confusing. It suggests that this gear is used primarily for casting *bait*, which is something alive or once was. Bass fishermen frequently use the word "bait" interchangeably with "lure," and that word tells us that the item the fish is supposed to grab is an artificial. It might be clearer if we simply called this revolving-spool reel with matching rod and line, *casting* tackle.

Casting reels are basically winches which revolve when line is payed out, or when the handle is cranked to retrieve the bait/lure. Such reels started out as simple mechanisms a couple of hundred years ago, but today's reels are marvels of complex design. If properly adjusted, most casting reels on the market today do their jobs well with a minimum of maintenance and keep on doing it for years. Drag mechanisms and antireverse systems that prevent the awful consequences of a backlash are efficient to the point of being almost foolproof. With a few hours of practice, almost anyone can toss a lure over a

hundred feet and come reasonably close to dropping that lure into a ten-foot circle.

Casting reels and appropriate rods for them are ideally suited for tossing lures (a.k.a. plugs) and some live baits. This is the tackle usually seen in the hands of bass fishermen—and for good reason. No other type of tackle is capable of such a high degree of accuracy. A good caster can put a lure into a gallon bucket at fifty feet. For casting into tiny pockets guarded by limbs and brush along lake shores this sort of reel is tops.

Where trout are concerned, casting reels are valuable for casting large lures accurately. Much of the time, however, smaller lures are required for trout which are better cast with a spinning outfit.

Lures weighing more than a quarter ounce can be cast well with modern casting reels. A lot of trout have been caught with such gear and more could be. While it's not considered traditional, casting reels may be the best choice for medium to large rivers. For big trout, steelhead, and Pacific salmon, these reels offer the advan-

Modern low-profile casting reels are equipped with magnetic spools that eliminate annoying tangles.

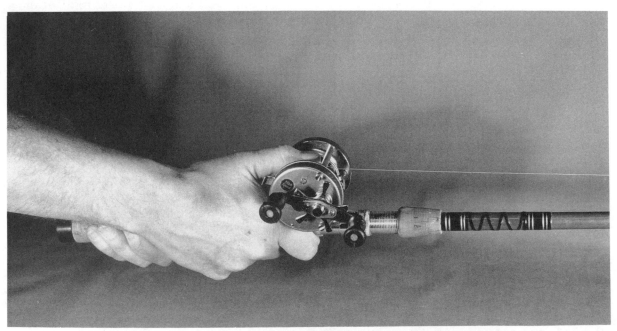

If a lot of boat fishing is done, reels with larger handles and more line capacity are useful. That big handle comes in handy when cold weather requires gloves.

The more traditional "round" casting reels are ideally suited for two-handed casting. Just like the golfers practice their shots on the lawn, anglers should work on their technique during the off-season as well.

tage of a good drag system, ample line capacity, and versatility. They're versatile because, should trolling be required, casting reels excel in this department.

In lakes and ponds where trolling is the standard approach, casting reels are the best choice for most anglers. It's easy to pay out line as the lure is being dropped to trolling depths, and the level-wind bar on nearly every casting reel makes cranking line back on the spool trouble-free. While reels vary in their buttons and controls, it's usually a matter of flipping a switch to release line. Turning the handle a half revolution re-engages the gear mechanism.

Setting up your casting reel for fishing consists of adjusting the spool tension and the drag mechanism. Different weight lures usually require a change in spool tension, and having it right will make casting much easier. It's done by allowing the lure to dangle from the tip of the rod with about six inches of line between it and the tip. Begin with the spool-tension adjustment set tightly. Loosen it slowly until the lure begins to drop in slow motion. Try a practice cast. If the reel spool turns too fast and line tends to override, tighten the spool a bit more. If the lure casts sluggishly, reduce the tension.

When casting reels were less sophisticated,

casters talked about an "educated thumb." It was necessary to keep the thumb of the casting hand bearing lightly on the revolving reel spool in order to prevent backlash or override. It's still necessary to begin a cast with the thumb on the reel spool, after the spool-release button has been pushed, but magnetic and other tension controls do almost all of the delicate adjusting for you. When learning to cast, it's still best to keep a light touch on the reel spool in case you want to stop a misdirected try.

The best way to learn how to use a casting reel is at the elbow of an expert. As with all kinds of casting, watching and doing are the best ways to learn. But if you don't have a nearby instructor, study the illustrations and the motions needed. It's not that difficult. As we've already noted, casting reels of today are light years ahead of yesterday's in ease of operation and efficiency.

In the photographs you'll note reels of several sizes with a wide range of handle designs and profiles. Competition is intense in all areas of tackle manufacture and reels are not unlike automobiles. Some new feature, new color, new size, or completely new design hits the market almost every year, and it hurries the angler to keep up with it. A representative selection of what's available appears here, but it does not include every reel. Nor does it constitute an endorsement. I do, however, consider all reels pictured to be good values and trustworthy gear.

Prices of casting reels range from under $30 to $200. That's quite a spread to be sure; as with most mechanical items, you usually get what you pay for. A solid "feel" when a reel is held in the hand and the handle rotated a few times is amazingly evident even to the novice. Loose, wobbling spools and handles, screws that don't fit well, sloppy paint or metal-plating jobs are obvious to everyone. Quality and what the tackle makers call "good cosmetics" are identifiable in the kind of reel you ought to buy. Low-profile reels, those that sit close to the reel seat and handle, are the trend today. They're more comfortable to use and are highly efficient. With some careful shopping you should find a good one for about $70 or less.

The literature in the reel box will tell you how much line of various diameters, or pound-test, can be cranked onto the spool. The line capacity is important if you're going to be doing a lot of deep trolling or casting heavy lures for lake trout, or have some special requirements. Most casting reels, even the very small ones will hold plenty of 6- to 12-pound-test line.

Which Line to Use

Unless you're already a whiz at casting and are highly skilled at handling big fish on light line, don't consider putting anything less than 6-pound test on your new reel. That's about as light as one can go and have some peace of mind when you hook a larger trout or salmon on a sizable lure. Six- or 8-pound test casts well, and you can put a lot of it on the reel. On the high side, any line testing heavier than 12 pound is excess baggage for the opposite reasons. Heavier line does not cast as well, may spook some cautious fish, and cuts down severely on line capacity. There's another subtle, though highly important, reason for using lighter line with certain lures. Some swimming-type lures and not a few others are extremely line sensitive. Attach a too-heavy line to them and the lure action is affected. They must "swim" freely in order to wobble suggestively. (Details, details. Attention to them will help us all catch more fish.)

Most of the time I choose 10-pound-test monofilament for my casting reel. It can cast 3-inch lures, trolls deep, and doesn't hamper the movement of live baits. For steelhead, salmon, and large trout in rivers I might go up to 12 pound. For trolling in deep lakes or for use with downriggers, 15 or 17 might be selected because snapping the line in and out of the downrigger clips causes extra wear and tear. For this reason, when fishing action is fast and furious it's a good idea to check your line carefully after every fish; remove any section of line that is nicked or feels rough. Yes, it takes time to do it but it's good insurance.

Huge Chinook salmon, those over 40 pounds, are the only salmon or trout that should ever require line testing over 20 pounds. If it makes you feel better, spool on some heavier monofilament if you find yourself in the salt chuck. A good reel with a smooth drag will make up for heavier line . . . if the angler doesn't try to overpower the fish. Remember, you'll be on the receiving end of more strikes with lighter line than with heavy stuff.

TROLLING AND DOWNRIGGER REELS

The extensive use of downriggers in the Great Lakes and many other waters has created another class of reels. Because very little actual casting is done when trolling with downriggers, there is no need for complex gearing and spool adjustments. Smoothness of operation and reliable drag mechanisms are more important. So are line capacity and sheer ruggedness.

These same requirements are what's needed by saltwater anglers who troll for the heavyweights such as marlin, sharks, swordfish, and tuna. Reels used for this purpose take a savage beating and must be well built in order to survive many seasons. Not surprisingly, these are among the most expensive of all reels. The magnificent Penn Internationals, the Daiwa Sealine Tournaments, the Finnor Tycoons, and a few others are representative of these top-drawer products. If

Large capacity trolling reels that resemble fly reels are rapidly gaining a place on many boats equipped with downriggers. They're simple to use and extremely rugged.

your budget will stand several hundred dollars for a reel go for one. It's a lifetime investment for a freshwater angler, but the rub is, for downrigging or regular trolling, a properly equipped boat needs three or more of them. We're talking serious commitment here!

Most reel makers offer standard revolving-spool reels at much lower prices, somewhat under $80, and in nearly all cases quality is high. Of course, trolling can be done with almost any sort of reel, but the stress that trolling gear is subjected to is unusual punishment for casting or spinning reels. If you expect to be doing a lot of trolling, then a trolling reel is the right thing to have.

Fortunately, there is an inexpensive alternative available today in the form of downrigger reels patterned after fly reels. The Australians and the British were probably the first to use a fly reel for trolling. They simply chose a rugged, large-frame fly reel, wound on line and went trolling. Refinements followed and what resulted were the Alvey trolling reel from Australia and the large spool Hardys from England. American makers such as Zebco and Mitchell countered with similar models and they perform equally well. Currently selling for under $75, reels of this type are marvels of simplicity, have efficient drags, great capacities and are easy to operate.

Why won't any kind of fly reel work as well as those designed for trolling? Well, some will, particularly those made of solid aluminum bar stock, but fly reels are designed to be used on lighter rods, hold the thicker fly lines and wear smaller handles. Fly reel spools are usually thinner and won't stand the strain of being wound full of monofilament line. Winding a couple hundred yards or more of monofilament line on a light metal or synthetic spool may break it.

CASTING RODS

The basic casting rod for trout, if the situation calls for such gear, ought to be 5½ or 6 feet long with a medium action. For casting a wide variety of lures and baits, the action should be a little on the "quick" side—that is, the tip should bend

rather smartly when the rod is flexed so as to toss lures at high velocity. Such a rod shouldn't bend very much until some force is applied. It's a good compromise if trout of many sizes may be encountered. The flexible tip—say, the first 12 inches or so—will bend at the rush of a small fish and the reserve power in the butt is always there if you hook something of trophy proportions. Fortunately, most rod manufacturers build such a stick.

I'd like to see at least five guides on my casting rod; six wouldn't be out of place. The more guides on a rod (up to a point) the more evenly the rod bends under pressure. A handle long enough to allow two-handed casting is also an important consideration, if you're going to fish long hours and you don't have the strength of a

For trolling or casting larger lures, a conventional casting rod performs well for lake and river fishing. The choice is wide, with graphite or graphite-glass composites leading the list of materials.

Many expert casters use a two-handed grip that beginners would do well to emulate. It's a less tiring way to cast and more accurate as well.

weight lifter. Two-handed casting is much less tiring.

Whatever the handle material, make sure it feels comfortable in your hand before you lay down the money. A fat, hand-filling handle may feel okay at first, but chances are it'll soon become cramping and difficult to manage. If the handle is cork, the preferred material, some work with sandpaper can adjust it to fit your hand.

This basic casting rod can be used for deep jigging, trolling, and almost any sort of live-bait fishing, as well as for casting lures. Ideally, a shorter, stiffer rod would be better for deep trolling and jigging, and a longer, more flexible rod would be preferred for downrigger trolling or live-bait fishing. Ah, but that's the beauty of this fishing game—there's always one more rod we need!

Casting rods made of split bamboo or metal

are out of the picture today, and all-glass-fiber rods are beginning to fade as well. Graphite and graphite/glass composites pretty much dominate the market and probably will for many years. Graphite is light, responsive, durable, and cheaper than it was ten years ago. Practically all makers are using it now in one degree or another. That's not to say that rods made totally with glass fibers aren't any good. They certainly are and millions of them are in use every day and will be for a long time. I have several glass rods I wouldn't part with.

Choosing the right graphite or graphite/glass composite is easy; a host of makers have just the thing. Studying the photos will show you what to look for. Examine the wrappings on the guides, the fit and finish of the hardware, and enlist the services of a fishing friend in helping you to make a decision. Install the reel you intend to use and test the way it feels in your hand. Remember, you'll be extending the thumb for line control on casting or spincast reels. Can you reach the reel with that thumb? If not, consider another rod . . . or another reel.

For deep trolling or jigging with heavy lures when seeking lake trout in fifty feet or more of water, a shorter, more powerful rod is needed. Heavy sinkers, jigs, and trolling lures will force the rod to flex, thus making it feel more responsive. Such a rod will not cast lures well: the force required to toss a live bait will probably tear the bait from the hook. When you get a hook-up in deep water, the power of the shorter rod will be much appreciated.

DOWNRIGGER RODS

Rods for downrigger trolling should be longer, 6 feet or more, and have a more flexible tip, but sufficient power in the butt. The rod is bent to accommodate attaching the line to the downrigger weight and should snap back smartly in order to hook the fish. Once this operation is seen, the advantages of this sort of rod will be immediately apparent.

Over the past ten years, rods designed for fishing extremely light lines when after larger trout and salmon have become quite popular. Called "noodling" rods because the action is very soft, these highly flexible shafts made practical what some anglers believed to be stunt fishing.

In some fishing circles, catching the largest possible fish on the smallest diameter line is the goal. There are two basic ways to go about this. One either uses a short, light rod with a small reel and hopes for the best or a long noodle rod.

The dynamics involved with the long, soft-action rod offer a better chance with lines testing 6 pounds or less. As a large fish runs, jumps, and pulls, the long, thin rod bends in a long arc that does not put a great deal of strain on the light line. No matter how hard the fish pulls, the shock of the battle is absorbed by the long rod and the drag of the reel, which is adjusted to release line at the slightest pull. Extremely large fish can be subdued with noodle rods; it just takes a little longer. (Successful fishing with such a rod requires that the reel have an extremely smooth drag.) Noodle rods are perfect for fishing with live baits, salmon eggs, and lures with small hooks that will stick in a fish's mouth without great pressure being exerted. It's a fun way to fish!

Trolling rods, particularly those used with down-rigger gear, must have longer handles in order to fit well in the rod holders. This Great Lakes chinook salmon struck a diving-type lure.

Rods for spincast reels should be selected with the same criteria in mind. The rod that functions well with casting reels will do the same with spincast reels.

LEADERS

In saltwater, where a number of species are armed with sharp dentures there is a good reason for using leaders of single-strand or braided wire. Wire leaders are unnecessary, however, when fishing for trout and salmon. When trolling for large trout or salmon, a leader heavier than the line spooled on the reel is needed at times. This is particularly true when a fish is to be released. If you're fishing with 6- or 8-pound test and a fish of 20 pounds or more is at boat side, handling it on light line can be a problem. You can grasp a thicker leader and have better control during the unhooking process.

A 6-foot leader is usually long enough for most trolling, and 10 feet is about as much as is ever needed. For casting, a leader that's about the same length as the rod is about right. If it's any longer, the knot connecting line and leader will prevent you from reeling in the fish close enough for netting. Various ways to attach leaders are shown in Chapter 12.

BRAIDED LINES

These lines are made, as the name implies, by braiding individual strands of nylon or Dacron into lines of different diameters and pound-tests. Linen, cotton, and silk are no longer used to make braided lines. These lines are strong and take knots well. They do absorb more water than monofilament and of course, being opaque instead of transparent, are more visible. Some anglers who troll a great deal like braided lines because they don't stretch as much as mono. Braided line has virtually no "memory" when spooled or stored on reels and so casts smoothly from revolving-spool (casting) reels. Braided line has not been used on spinning reels for many years.

HOW TO CAST

Casting with a revolving-spool reel is essentially the same as with a spinning or spincasting reel. The rod is flexed on the backstroke by the weight of the lure; then driven forward on the downstroke, the lure powered by the wrist and the reverse flex of the rod. However, handling this type of reel requires attention to the following details:

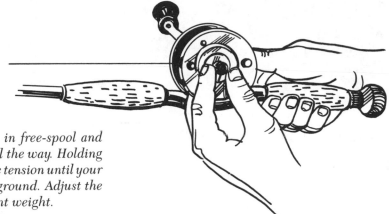

1

To prepare to cast, put the reel in free-spool and tighten the spool tension knob all the way. Holding the rod level, gradually lessen the tension until your lure slowly pulls the line to the ground. Adjust the tension for each lure of a different weight.

2

Hold the rod with the reel handles up and your thumb on the spool. The reel should still be in free-spool. When the rod reaches the 11 o'clock position on the forward cast, raise your thumb so the lure can pull line off the revolving spool. When the lure nears its target, brake its flight by thumb pressure.

3

To retrieve the lure, hold the rod as shown, between the first and second fingers of your left hand and the line between your thumb and first finger.

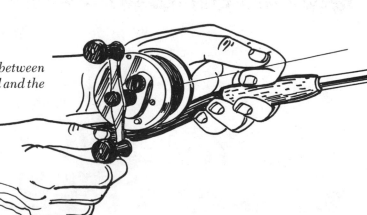

5

The Trout in the Stream

All trout are concerned with three basic goals. Trout don't think as humans do, but nonetheless they must eat, reproduce, and escape predators if they are to survive as individuals and as a species. They attend to this instinctively. These three goals are connected with an overall desire for comfort. Just as we seek warmth in winter and shade or air conditioning in summer, trout are more or less active depending on the surrounding water temperature. For most stream trout, the ideal comfort zone is 58 to 65 degrees. Brook trout and lake trout prefer somewhat cooler water, and browns may choose warmer surroundings. No trout, however, will remain in water that rises to much over 70 degrees for long periods. If water temperature reaches 75, most trout will probably die within a day or so if they have no escape. Trout seek deeper water in winter and midsummer, because it remains more consistent. The obvious angling tip here is to fish deeper during very cool or very warm weather.

Fishing is usually better during early morning or late evening hours because fish feel more secure. Overhead light is not casting shadows then. This may not be a factor in lakes and ponds but it certainly is in streams and rivers. Here, trout will more often be found close to or underneath rocks, ledges, overhanging banks, or in deeper water if such hiding places are not available.

When an abundance of food, such as a hatch of insects, is in progress they'll lose some of their wariness and venture into the shallows to dine on the bounty. But even then, they usually have an escape route planned and will dart for cover when spooked or hooked. It's no accident that trout head for overhanging brush or underwater rocks when hooked. It's their natural escape plan and it often works . . . to our dismay.

While general temperature ranges can be said to be ideal or poor for trout fishing, we must always remember that trout are highly opportunistic. This is particularly true of wild trout that have not seen the inside of a hatchery truck or stocked fish that have been in the stream for some time. They must eat when natural food is available. There are months when certain seasonal foods, such as aquatic insects, grass-

Overhanging vegetation is a sure bet to shelter trout in any stream. Try to drift bait, lures, or flies as close to the greenery as possible.

hoppers, and flying ants, are abundant. It follows that an imitation or the real thing is the right lure or bait at those moments. Find the fish, toss the right thing in their direction, and success should follow. Right? Well, sometimes. Varying water temperatures in the same section of water can affect the outcome.

Most trout streams that do not have their beginnings at one huge underground spring or are formed by the tailwaters of a dam, rise or drop in volume and temperature every day. While these changes are nearly imperceptible at times, they can affect the fishing. Noticeable changes in flow, such as high and muddy or low and clear water, will affect it in profound ways.

A good general rule is to fish the edges of fast-moving sections of water or the eddies and quiet places when water is high or discolored. Trout can swim through very swift water, but for rest-

ing and feeding they'll take the easier current every time. They'll be in the eddies and edges for another reason. That's where the minnows will be, because these small fish cannot hold a position in swift-moving water. Land creatures such as earthworms, grubs, ants, and other insects will also be near stream edges after a hard rain or periods of high water. Trout will always follow the easy-to-gather food.

Another rule of thumb that proves true more often than not is that very warm or very cold water causes trout to move to deep pools and shaded areas. Deep pools are warmer in the winter and early spring and cooler in the summer. They are because air and water temperatures are converse factors then. If the air temperature is a chilly 42 degrees, 55-degree water at the bottom of a deep pool is warm. If the air is a sizzling 90 degrees that same 55 degrees is

On any fast-flowing stream, a pool immediately below a falls or swiftly moving white water is usually productive. Trout hold in the pool, waiting for food to be washed over the falls.

If you encounter sections of white water in a stream, fish the edges of the currents, in the slick, dark water or, as in the previous photo, the pools below the rapids.

cool. You won't see much surface activity on a trout stream when the air temperature is that warm. The water temperature near the surface won't be 90, but it will probably be in the 70s, and that's too hot for most trout.

TROUT FOODS

There are three groups of natural foods that are most important to all species of trout: minnows of many sorts and the young of larger fish species, including their own; aquatic insects and crustaceans; and land-born creatures such as insects, worms, and beetles. Trout have been observed eating some vegetable matter and a wide variety of small mammals and birds, but the bulk of their diet consists of creatures that live in or near the water.

It's impossible to make an overall statement about which natural food is most important to trout. Availability of certain insects, minnows, worms, crayfish, etc., varies from stream to stream and lake to lake. Trout are opportunists and feed on the most available foods. Therefore, fishing with a natural bait, or an imitation of it, that happens to be common in the water at hand is the correct approach.

To the nonangler's eye most waters don't appear to be as abundant with life as they usually are. There are trout there, but what else? Minnow species number in the hundreds, but among the most common are the bottom-dwelling sculpins, and minnows that travel in small schools, such as blacknose dace, common chubs, various shiners, and suckers. A trout will capture and eat almost any small fish that's less than a fourth of its own length. Since most common baitfish don't grow to be much more than a few

The protruding rock formation at the right of the photo is the kind of overhanging cover that trout prefer. This angler has just hooked one there.

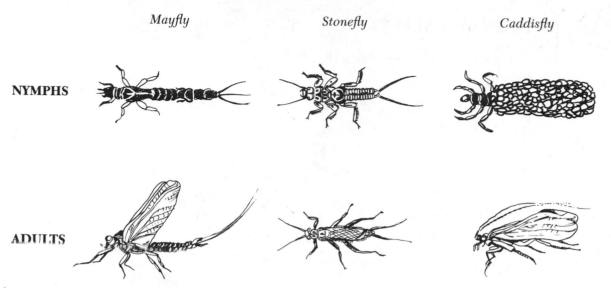

Mayfly   *Stonefly*   *Caddisfly*

NYMPHS

ADULTS

Most prevalent insects found in trout streams are the mayfly, caddisfly, and stonefly. These are the nymphal and adult forms, both imitated by artificial flies.

inches long, it follows that lures and flies needn't be excessively large. Where trout are bigger, as in lakes or deep rivers, lures must be larger; but even here, any lure or bait longer than 5 inches will seldom be needed. Most popular casting, trolling, and spinning lures are designed to represent small fish. So are the elongated flies known as streamers.

Trout of all sizes are fond of crayfish and eat many of them because they're easier to catch than a fleeing minnow. In streams and rivers where crayfish are plentiful, larger trout, those of 20 inches or more, tend to concentrate on them. Since crayfish are more active during the dark hours, using them as bait pays off well during late evening and early morning.

In the vast majority of trout streams, the many species of aquatic insects make up a huge part of the trout's diet. The three most important insect groups are the mayflies, caddisflies and stoneflies. These are the insects that are most often suggested by the many fly patterns that have been created, primarily, for trout. For many anglers the study of these insects becomes as fascinating as the fishing itself. While some knowledge of these creatures can certainly help one become a better angler, a general understanding of their life cycle is adequate. The Latin names for these insects are difficult to pronounce and even more difficult to remember. The March Brown mayfly, for example, has been tagged with *Stenonema vicarium*. The trout don't know this, nor do they care.

There are many subtle differences in how aquatic insects are conceived and grow, but what's most important to know is that there are two stages in which they are important to the trout. Mayflies and stoneflies transform themselves into adults from the nymphal stage by erupting from a thin sheath of "skin" much like a crayfish or lobster does. When the mayfly nymph is ready to hatch it swims to the surface and escapes from it's nymphal shuck rather quickly. With some species, this hatching process is almost instantaneous, with the winged adults fairly popping into the air. A few others, such as the large green drake, flop and flutter for several minutes in an attempt to become airborne. This action usually triggers the trout into a feeding spree. Mayflies hatch on the surface whereas stoneflies must crawl onto a rock or shoreline in order to shed their skins. The basic difference between mayflies and stoneflies is the configuration of the wings. Mayfly wings are erect and

LIFE CYCLE OF A MAYFLY

1. *The female deposits her eggs on the water.*

2. *The eggs sink to the bottom of the stream and adhere to underwater rocks or logs.*

3. *In about thirty days, the eggs hatch into nymphs, which cling to underwater vegetation, rocks, and logs. In one year, the nymphs hatch, emerging on the surface as winged flies called duns.*

4. *The duns fly to streamside brush and trees, change into the spinner, or imago, form and return to the stream to mate. When the mating is accomplished, and the female deposits her eggs, the spinners die on the surface and are called spentwings. Then the cycle begins again.*

slanted slightly towards the tail. Stonefly wings are elongated and folded on top of the body when the insect is not flying.

Caddisfly larvae protect themselves as juveniles by building cases around themselves. These cases are formed of tiny stones, bits of wood, and other minute debris, and held together by a secretion manufactured in the insect's body. When feeding on caddis larvae, trout swallow case and all. This is one of the reasons small stones and sticks are frequently in a trout's stomach.

By examining the underside of rocks and sticks in most trout streams, it's quite easy to find nymphs of mayflies and stoneflies and the little cases of caddis. The caddis cases are not difficult to identify once you begin to notice the moving head of the larva sticking slightly out of the open end of the case. Caddis adults are erratic flyers and dip and dive to the water in fits and starts. There are several subspecies in many colors.

Mayfly and stonefly nymphs appear quite similar to the casual observer, but a closer examination will reveal that mayfly nymphs have longer tails, and all six of the legs are attached to the body at or near the thorax, or center portion. Stonefly legs (six also) are evenly spaced from just behind the head to the beginning of the abdomen or rear portion. It's worth spending an hour or so looking for nymphs and larvae. It's not difficult to spot the differences and will lead to an understanding of why there are so many fly patterns.

There are many exceptions to every statement made about any aspect of trout fishing (which makes it so interesting). But it is generally true that insects appear on a trout stream in a certain sequence. They do because all insects are programmed to hatch and breed at specific times. Many books on fly fishing contain emergence charts listing the dates certain insects will (or should) appear. While this information is useful, the trout are not aware of it and many other conditions can alter the dates considerably. High water, extreme temperatures, lack of sunlight, and other factors can bring certain hatches on sooner or later. Of more importance to the novice is to know that the first insects of spring are usually smaller and darker. As the season progresses, the flies become larger and lighter in shade. During late summer and early fall it's back to smaller and darker flies again.

In the chapter on fly fishing, a "starter" list of flies is offered, and by studying these patterns at the tackle shop you'll see the differences in color and silhouette.

SPAWNING

All of the trouts, chars, and salmons can be migratory to a degree in any brook, stream, or river. There are migrations of a sort in still ponds and lakes where lake trout and brook trout move to the shallow edges for spawning chores during the late autumn months. The freshwater to saltwater travels of the steelhead trout and Atlantic and Pacific salmons are well known, as are those of the sea-run browns of Europe and the "coasters," or sea-going brook trout, of North America. Much less known is the fact that there is considerable movement or migration in many trout streams that don't have clear access to the ocean.

Toward the end of summer or the early days of autumn most brown and brook trout begin to get "broody." They must sense the approach of spawning and are taken by an urge to find a suitable area for reproduction chores. In some small brooks this migration may merely consist of moving to another part of the same pool or a few yards upstream. In larger streams the annual trek to spawning areas may involved thousands of yards or several miles. The causes of this urge to move are not fully understood, but a drop in water temperature, reduced amount of sunlight, expanding egg sacs are undoubtedly part of it. A warm fall might delay this migration and a cool one could speed it up. High or low water could also affect the timing. But the migration will come sooner or later, and such movement frequently brings some fantastic angling to pools where previously there were no fish at all. In many rivers of the northeastern U.S., pools that had been nearly barren during August can suddenly become highly productive in mid-September.

As with all pre-spawning trout, their protective instincts, particularly those of the male fish, cause them to strike at flies and lures that would not interest them at other times of the year. This is the time to tie on a flashy streamer fly, a big White Wulff dry fly, or a hot-orange spinning lure. Forget matching the hatch—what's needed here is something to make them mad!

A conservation note about fishing for trout in the act of spawning: In many states the trout fishing season is closed during the peak of spawning activity. In others it is not, and that presents an ethical (or perhaps an ethical/environmental) question. Where put-and-take angling prevails, that is, where most of the trout caught are hatchery raised, fishing all year doesn't matter much. Where a significant number of trout are native or stream-bred fish, angling during the spawning season can be detrimental to future seasons. Catching some of the smaller and precocious male trout does little harm. There will always be enough aggressive males around to handle fertilization chores. Wading into and destroying spawning redds is far more serious and can be done without the angler realizing that he's doing something wrong.

If you see spawning activity or locate a nest, or redd, don't fish for trout engaged in the mating ritual and don't wade in that area until that activity ends.

With few exceptions, the trout and salmon of the east spawn in the fall and the trout of the west spawn in the spring. Various strains of Pacific salmon can be spring and fall spawners, which is one of nature's ways of assuring a continuing population should a serious drought or flood occur. To a degree, all fish stagger their spawning times with the same result—survival of the species.

While there are many subtleties among the spawning characteristics of trout and salmon, they are of small interest to most anglers. It is sufficient to have a general understanding of the spawning act and how long it takes for fish to reach catchable size.

Watching a female brown trout "build" her nest is a major streamside thrill. Surprisingly, not many trout anglers have been unfortunate enough to see nest making, mating, or spawning, for the nest is not easy to spot and the spawning hen fish is very well camouflaged. The backs of male and female trout are chameleonlike, but during the spawning season this phenomenon is even more evident. The females' top side will be precisely the shade of the nest gravel. Even the male fish, while brilliant on their flanks and bellies, will be nearly as well disguised on their backs.

As the fall season progresses and the water temperature and other conditions seem right, the mature female brown trout begins to search for a nesting site. It appears that most redds are located where water velocity is between one to two feet per second and six inches to two feet deep. The experts disagree on this and trout in different waters probably do too—but they know what they're looking for. If the current and depth feel right, the hen begins to hollow out a spot in the gravel by swishing her tail back and forth and turning on her side to kick in a downward direction. Eventually, she'll form a craterlike depression that will be continuously washed clean by a steady current.

All of this nest-making activity is bound to attract the attention of a male trout and usually several of them. A particular male assumes the husband role and begins to work overtime trying to chase the other males away from his chosen bride. He can get hurt doing this. Fighting males sometimes die from their wounds, and it's not unusual at spawning time to see several males around a redd with chewed-off tails, torn fins, damaged or missing eyes, and fatal skin punctures. Some heal for another season and some don't.

When serious spawning takes place, the hen drops low into the nest and begins to vibrate, kicking with her tail and opening her mouth in a yawning or gaping attitude. The excited male wiggles against her lateral line, and he also opens his mouth in an extended way. This touching and wiggling stimulates the female, and she ejects some eggs. The male immediately discharges some milt (sperm) and the eggs are fertilized as they drop into the nest. The female swishes some gravel over the nest to hide the eggs from predators, and the males dashes about, at the ready, to chase off other would-be suitors.

In the case of a small female, the spawning act will be over in a day or so. A large trout will pass through several egg-laying flurries that may last for five days or more. Subsequent eggs will go on top of the last batch and they will also be covered. The minimum size for sexual maturity varies greatly from stream to stream. I've watched trout as small as 6 inches drop eggs and males as small as 4 inches show sexual prowess, but 12 inches is more the average.

About 400 eggs to the pound of fish will be deposited, their size relative to the size of the females. This size difference may have some influence on how fast the offspring mature. Each egg will form an eye in about thirty days, and after two more months the tiny fish will leave the nest to be on their own. If all goes well for them, a year of growing should see the 1-inch alevins become 4-inch fingerlings.

Life for a trout is filled with perils from egg to adult. Other fish eat them at all stages. Kingfishers are fond of them in the 1- to 4-inch range. Blue herons, snapping turtles, and water snakes can easily handle trout up to a foot long; beyond that length, ospreys, raccoons, bears, otters, and humans take up the chase. Floods, droughts, and pollution of all kinds take a heavy toll as well. Usually no more than 2 percent of all trout eggs deposited in a wild environment survive their first year.

In spite of the hazards facing wild trout, enough can survive to offer excellent fishing in streams that remain relatively free of human-induced pollution. They've been doing it for centuries and will continue to do so with just a little help from their friends.

HATCHERY TROUT

Eventually, every angler reaches the stage where he places native or wild trout on a piscatorial pedestal. This is understandable. In fact, much good has come from the crusading done by stalwarts who fussed enough to see many excellent trout streams returned to their former glories. But if trout fishing is to be enjoyed by the millions who pursue the game, it follows that even more millions of trout must be reared in hatcheries. By the tens of millions they are. From federal, state, and private hatcheries, brook, brown, rainbow, and an assortment of hybrid trout are stocked in many North American waters that would not have trout otherwise.

In some streams, stocked trout supplement the native supply; in others, hatchery trout are the only fish. Anglers who are fortunate enough to cast only to wild trout will wonder how a total population of stocked trout could possibly provide a sporting situation. Dumb fish? Too easy to catch? Hardly. Many creel surveys have proven that hatchery fish, if they survive opening day, can become fully as difficult to catch as stream-reared trout. Perhaps trout can't learn as humans do, but they certainly avoid things with hooks in them in a seemingly intelligent manner.

TROUT IN SMALL STREAMS

For the purposes of this book a small stream will be classified as any flowing water that is thirty feet or under in average width. Of course, this definition includes some very tiny rivulets where trout may be found; some of them less than three feet wide. To the beginner, it might sound like total craziness to consider trout of catchable proportions being found in streams that small. It is well documented that trout weighing more than four pounds have been caught in streams that were barely deep enough to cover such a fish's back. Such behemoths are far from the rule, but that's the beauty of small-stream angling; you just never know what's going to turn up next!

The chief difference between small streams in civilized and remote areas lies in the wariness of the trout. This is true regardless of trout species. The numbers of predators (man included) has a direct bearing on their spookiness, but this factor aside, just seeing the silhouette of an angler is enough to put small-stream trout into a panic.

Fishing a small meadow stream requires stealth and short casts. Heavy footfalls can send fish scurrying for cover. Try to keep as far from the bank as possible.

The alert novice soon discovers that to wade in or walk beside a small brook in a heavy-footed manner does not contribute to success. His only reward will be to see the wakes of darting fish running for cover, leaving the pool as empty as his bathtub. Approach any small-stream pool cautiously and *slowly*. This is the chiseled-in-stone rule for the experienced angler.

Unless high or discolored water masks one's silhouette, all fishing on small streams should be done in an upstream direction. This is because trout, all fish for that matter, lie in moving water with their heads directed into the current. They do so because they must in order to breath comfortably. Fish can be found facing downstream in certain pools, but careful observation will prove that some interruption in the flow has caused the current to flow backwards, forming what's known as an eddy. Because of these eddies and other oddities in small streams, each pool must be approached with some plan in mind. It's seldom possible to catch more than one fish from a particular pool without a wait in between. Therefore, we've got to make the most of our first chance.

A small brook is the best place to learn how to "read the water." While the knowledgeable angler appears to have the knack of casting to the right spot, he had to learn too. Small streams are pocket-size editions of larger rivers, and every possible configuration of bank and bottom is there in miniature.

Basically, trout prefer being reasonably close to some sort of overhead cover and will seldom lie far from it. The spots to concentrate on are those that are shaded by overhanging limbs,

Trees and brush hamper casting on small streams and force the angler to dangle and dabble his bait, lure, or fly in unconventional ways.

stumps, large rocks, or brushy banks. Deep pockets of water immediately below fast stretches, rapids, or waterfalls are also good lairs. Undercut banks and ledges are hotspots, as are log jams and extremely deep pools that appear darker than the rest of the water. If the small stream does not have many of these natural obstructions and features and flows at a more rapid pace, expect to find the trout immediately in front of and behind natural "Vs" in the current. These spots are called pocket water and are the places to cast. A few trips to a small brook are necessary to develop this "fish sense," but the learning is a lot of fun.

While trout in small brooks are nervous, if a natural bait, lure, or fly can be delivered quietly, the likelihood of a strike is great. The majority of small brooks are not as food rich as are much larger streams, so the fish in them are eager to

grab a bite whenever possible, and they aren't usually too fussy about what it is.

In general, the trout most frequently encountered in small streams east of the Mississippi are brook trout. The same holds true for most of eastern Canada and the upper Midwest. In the Rocky Mountain states the native fish can be either the rainbow or the cutthroat, and in the far West it'll probably be the rainbow. These are not rigid rules, since stocking of all trout species has been tried in most trout fishing regions. Some small brooks in North Carolina, for example, contain good populations of brown, rainbow, and brook trout. These can be self-sustaining populations and not annually stocked, hatchery-reared fish. The same holds true in the West, where the eastern brook trout and the European brown trout have been successfully introduced to hundreds of streams. There are differences

You may get mud and grass stains on your clothes, but approaching small brooks often requires strenuous work. This angler has lowered her profile and kept well back from the bank in order to fish a tiny brook.

A 10-inch native brookie is a commendable catch on most small streams, but larger fish may be there too. With abundant grass at stream-side, expect grasshoppers to be in the area. That's what caught this fish.

between the trout, of course, in physical appearance and food preferences, but in small brooks these differences are neutralized to a great extent.

TROUT IN LARGE STREAMS

A useful angler's definition of a *large* stream is one that he can cast across—or almost. This works out to mean flowing water between thirty and somewhat over a hundred feet in width. Since a hundred-foot cast is a mighty long one with fly tackle and longer than average with spin or casting tackle, any stream wider than that must be considered a river. In either case, bigger water presents a different set of situations when

This 16-inch brook trout proves that not all fish in small streams are pocket-sized. This one went for a Mickey Finn streamer.

In addition to catching a skillet full of pretty trout in a small brook, this angler also found some wild flowes to decorate his hat.

compared with small streams and brooks. In large streams, trout will be more widely distributed, somewhat less cautious, and probably larger. The wider stream offers the opportunity to make longer casts with all types of tackle. The angler will also discover that hip boots or waders are useful.

As noted, when fishing small brooks, the best approach is to face upstream. On larger waters, however, it's not always possible to do this nor is it the best plan. You have more water to "work" with, and in order to fish it thoroughly you'll have to cast in all directions.

In general, most streams follow nature's traditional architecture and are laid out in a combination of fast rippling shallows and deeper pools—one after the other. The common angling procedure is to bypass the swift water and concentrate on the pools. Fair enough, because the most and biggest trout will probably be in the pools. Overlooked by many anglers are the irregularities, some subtle, some obvious, that have been created by fallen logs, boulders, undercut banks, and conflicting currents. Such natural obstructions and configurations are attractive to trout and to become a better-than-average trout fisherman you have to learn how to "read the water." This is important in today's angling world, because as more people come to the sport, the obvious trout holding places will be more heavily patrolled.

By studying the typical pool drawings, you can visualize most fishing situations. Regardless of your skill as a caster or your ability to choose the correct lure or bait, delivering your offering to a likely trout-holding spot is 95 percent of the game. Some of the best trout anglers in the world are not expert casters or highly competent waders. They don't own the best or most expensive tackle. What they do know, is *where* to cast, *when* to cast, and *what* to do *after* they cast. That's what trout fishing is all about.

Sample Pool A

A most common configuration occurs when the streambed drops rapidly. A section of rapids leads into a long pool that fades from a swift-moving current into a placid glide that's known as "slick" water. There are a few exposed rocks at the fast end of this typical pool and a belt of deep water (indicated by dark shading) in the center of the quieter water. There is also an undercut bank on the off side of the stream. The deep-water section becomes narrow as the pool leads into yet another shallow, rapid area.

The expected positions of trout in this kind of pool are indicated. They'll be there because they're conditioned to having food delivered to them in those locations, or because it's a good vantage point from which to watch for predators—anglers included.

POOL A

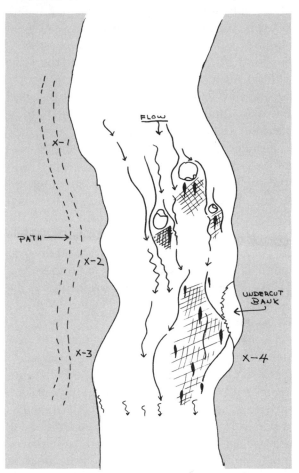

The spots indicated by X are preferred casting positions. Probable trout locations are marked by a fish silhouette. You'll seldom see trout when you're on the stream, but by studying these pool illustrations you'll know where the fish ought to be.

If you're moving downstream and using wet flies, streamer flies, a spinning lure, or natural bait of some kind, don't overlook the "pocket" water in front of and behind the exposed rocks. The trout in these locations have first chance at insects or other live creatures that come drifting by. Because of the swift water, they must grab whatever they're going to without much hesitation.

From position X-1 the boulders and rocks can be cast to effectively. Sunken lures and wet flies can be cast slightly beyond the leading edge of the rocks and retrieved diagonally. Some natural baits can be fished from this location but not all. X-1 is the ideal spot from which to fish a rigged minnow (see Chapter 6), but not the best location for drifting a worm. To fish around the rocks with worms and most other live bait, position X-2 is preferred. From there the bait can be dropped above the supposed hotspot and allowed to tumble naturally in the current.

From position X-2, the fish in the deeper water (indicated by shading) can be reached with sunken lures and flies. If you're traveling upstream, this position is the place to be when casting dry flies to those rocks at the head of the pool. The floating flies can be dropped slightly above the fish and allowed to drift naturally over them. The same advice applies to position X-3. This is a good casting location for the fish in the upper portion of the deep section, when dry flies are called for.

Depending on what you're fishing with, X-2 and X-3 can be equally good casting locations to reach the fish that are sticking close to that undercut bank. Generally, the sunken offerings are cast across and downstream and the floating flies are delivered upstream. But that undercut bank is a special place. Such a sheltered, shadowed spot is almost certain to be a "big" fish hideaway. If reaching the edge of the bank proves to be a longer cast than you can manage, it may be necessary to wade across the shallow end of the pool and have a try from X-4. From here, you can drop a bait practically on top of the hotspot or make a very short cast with a dry fly along the edge of the cutbank.

It's worth spending a few more words on these undercut banks. Most trout streams of all sizes have several, and all of them deserve more than passing attention. The largest trout in the stream are apt to be there, and if the right presentation is made, they're not nearly as difficult to catch as are trout in the middle of the stream.

The fish are under the bank because they've learned that this is fine protection from overhead predators such as herons, ospreys, kingfishers, and the like. They are extremely cautious about everything coming at them from the center of the pool but very "trusting" about food falling from the edge of the bank. This is why X-4 is usually the best place to operate from. Try to present fly, lure, or bait in a way that suggests it "just happened" to fall from the bank. And walk easy on top of that bank; heavy footfalls can vibrate through the rocks and soil and may tip off your presence.

Pool B

This is another common situation, with rippling water entering the pool in such a way that the main current flows toward a brush bank cutting a long, deep pocket beside it. A half-submerged log has been added to this illustration since it presents a typical obstruction that alters the flow. As with the undercut bank situation, the trout are drawn to the brushy bank because it offers overhead protection and quick escape hatches. There is the added attraction of worms, beetles, and other terrestrial insects that frequent such places and may fall into the water.

Again, the deepest water is indicated by dark cross hatches, and that's where the largest fish will be most of the time. A prolific hatch of floating insects may bring them out into the center of the pool, but an angler approaching from the right side will have to maintain a low profile or make a long cast to avoid spooking them. Most experienced trout anglers are not keen on wading when it's not absolutely necessary. This is particularly true when the water is low or extremely clear. The slightest bit of muddy or cloudy water is a clue to the trout that something is amiss. Assuming that the right side of the pool is shallow enough for easy wading, here's a situation where getting into the water *is* called for.

If you are fly fishing, from X-4, you should cast a dry fly into the center of the pool. Toss a short cast at first in order to pick up a willing taker that might be there and then gradually extend your casts toward the protected bank. Cast up and across, eventually coming as close to the brushy bank as possible.

Trout in such locations often hug the very roots of stream-side greenery. Thousands of trout have been caught by accident when an

POOL B

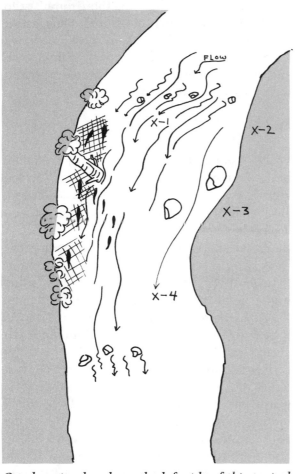

Overhanging brush on the left side of this typical pool is the obvious trout hangout. Position X-2 should be cast from before wading out to X-1, in order to avoid spooking the odd trout that may be closer to the fast water. Refer to text for more about this kind of pool.

errant cast put the fly into a tree, then jiggled loose to fall into the jaws of a waiting customer. The effect is perfect. It appears to the fish that something good to eat has just dropped from a limb. Creating such "accidents" is the mark of a well-traveled angler.

Continue casting from X-4 until you've reached your distance limit and then move on to X-3 and cover the rest of the bank area in the same way. Make some extra casts around the end

and on both sides of the extended log. Such an interruption in the flow is an excellent holding spot, and it's a good bet that the largest fish in the pool will be there.

From X-3, depending on distance, you may also be able to reach into the slightly faster water at the head of the pool. Some trout may be there trying to get a jump on the fish in the lower end of the pool as choice food drifts downstream. If you can't manage a decent float with a dry fly here, move to X-2 and allow the cast to move from the fast water into the pool.

If you're fishing downstream with wet flies, streamers, or bait, Pool B is best fished from X-2. Cast into the fast water to allow your offering to drift into the deeper areas. If you don't think you've covered the water in front of that half-sunken log adequately, wade to position X-1 and try a few more casts. But remember, wade carefully and try not to dislodge loose gravel or mud, otherwise you'll disturb the rest of the pool.

Fish the rest of the pool by moving to position X-3 and on to X-4, casting as close to the bank as possible and retrieving a wet fly, streamer, or spinning lure as seductively as you can manage. All forms of live and other baits should be allowed to drift along freely with the current.

Pool C

Another common but highly productive pool type occurs at the confluence of a stream entering a major river. Here food for the trout comes to them from two directions. It's also a protected spot; the constant flow from both steams meet to create a natural whirlpool during high-water periods. The resulting turbulence scoops out the stream bottom forming a deep pocket. Large, underwater boulders, too heavy for the current to dislodge, may be here. Even without boulders for cover, the deeper water alone offers protection that the trout feel comfortable with. The largest trout in most streams are quite likely to be in these junction locations.

With dry flies or live bait, the best approach is the same as with Pool B. Begin at X-3 or X-5 and cast into the shaded areas first. Then move to X-2 or X-4, depending on which side of the stream

POOL C

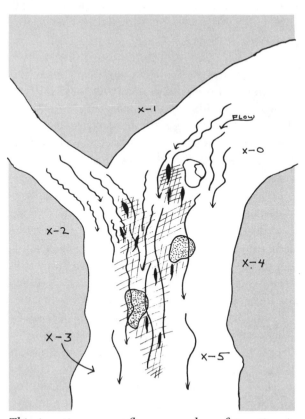

This junction or confluence pool configuration is quite common. It's an excellent place to fish streamers or spinning lures. Check the text for more on how to approach this type of stream.

you're on. Advance to X-1 and X-0, but if you're on the left side of the stream it will be necessary to wade across the incoming brook. Walk up the brook for some distance before crossing to avoid scaring the trout that may be lying with their noses in the brook current. The same holds true for wading out to position X-0. Do it cautiously. A lot of trout could be bunched up at the confluence and too much splashing around could "quiet" the pool for hours. For downstream angling with wet flies, streamers, lures, and drifting baits, reverse the casting position sequence.

Junction pools like this one come in many configurations and with combinations such as those found in Pools A and B. Low-water times and late summer may find confluence pools at

their most productive, because that's where most of the trout will be. They'll be there because the smaller, faster-flowing brook is frequently cooler than the main river—and trout prefer cool water. Such pools are usually deeper and hold more and larger fish when other pools temporarily lose their appeal.

Pool D

Pool D is not really a pool but rather a section of broken water, generally referred to as "pocket water." As with the other pool types illustrated, any or all of these configurations can and do occur on many trout streams. To be able to fish them well requires some skill in reading the water.

Regardless of the type of stream bottom, the water chemistry, or the available overhead light, the small depressions in the stream bottom will appear to be darker than their surroundings. The change in color may be quite subtle, but the surface texture is also a clue. It will be somewhat less ripply. It's extremely difficult to explain in words but by studying illustration D and then looking for such pockets when on the stream, the pocket water mystery should be easily solved. It's also a great help for the trout tyro to watch an experienced angler work the pockets with a floating fly. Wading carefully upstream, he casts accurately to each spot of dark holding water.

Accuracy in presentation is important when fishing broken water, as shown in "D." Immediately behind large rocks and boulders is a common trout-holding location, and not infrequently there will be a fish on the upstream side of such an obstruction. If the current is of the right velocity, a cushion of slower water will form there creating a feeding and resting spot. Because that spot will be a small one, fish holding there will probably not be big ones. They will also be forced to seize food in a hurry because the splitting current is fast. You must hit the leading edge of the pocket with your cast and then pick up the line and cast again. As a rule of thumb, six casts are enough on any spot of pocket water. If the fish is going to grab your offering it's most likely to do so on the first or second try.

POOL D

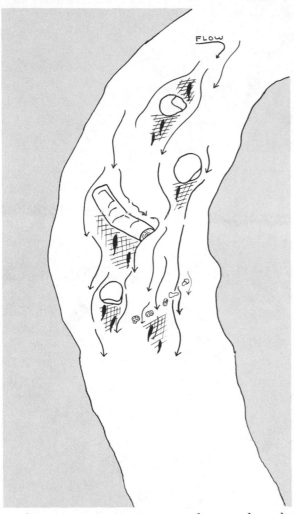

In this common stream situation, large rocks and a semisubmerged log provide a variety of holding spots for trout. Trout will usually be found on the downstream side of obstructions to the flow. No casting positions are indicated here. You decide where to fish from and then check the text to find out if you're right.

As I've noted before, fishing any stretch of water is sometimes difficult, if not impossible, to do without some wading. Broken water is one of these situations. Make every effort to fish such water with upstream casts. The more shallow pocket water doesn't offer much cover for the fish and the sight of your silhouette or dislodged debris floating over a spooky trout reduces chances for success.

It's not hair-splitting to avoid casting your shadow across the areas you intend to fish. Of course this is not always possible, but when a shadow can't be masked, keep a low profile and move slowly. A sure tip-off that identifies the experienced trout angler is his lack of sudden movements. He stalks the stream and calculates each move. Even his casting style is smooth and free of herky-jerky twitches. Such attention to details pays off.

Practically all stream situations and configurations are covered in the pool illustrations, and the only way to expand your knowledge of reading the water is to spend more time fishing. What a wonderful way of learning. The basic guidelines to be remembered are:

1. Don't wade unless it's necessary.
2. Make each cast as softly as possible, avoiding noisy *ker-plunks*.
3. If you must wade, do it gently without shuffling the rocks around or excess splashing. Plan each cast, fishing the near water first and the far water last.
4. Watch other experienced anglers and try to copy their tactics. Remember, every surgeon had to see a few appendectomies before he could manage a good one. Thank goodness.

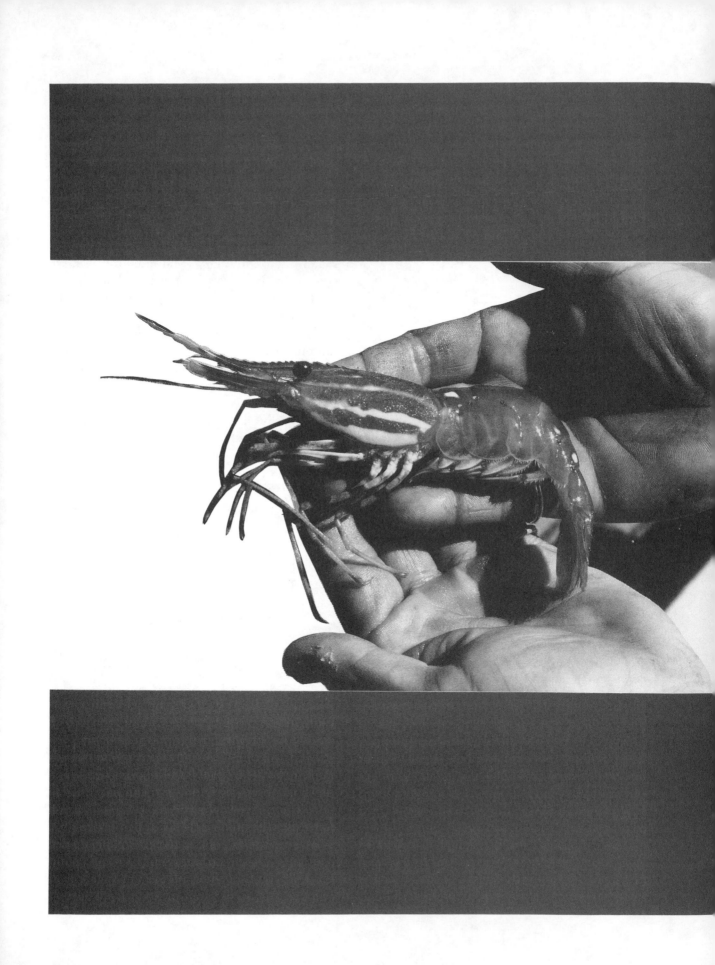

6

Fishing with Bait

Baitfishing is regarded as less than sporting by those who fish only with artificial lures and flies. But in certain waters and at certain times of the year, baitfishermen will be the only ones catching fish.

Baitfishing can be as simple as casting a live garden worm into a pool and waiting for a trout to take it. Millions of trout have been caught in this way, and millions more will be. But continued success with live bait is not the simple-minded pursuit some believe it to be. Fishing with live bait is the best way to learn about the habits of trout even if the eventual goal is to become a purist fly angler. No other fishing method teaches you as well how trout feed and behave. Baitfishing is also an excellent way to introduce beginners to the pleasures of fishing, because at the outset catching fish is more exciting than not catching them. If presented correctly, there is always *some* natural bait that a trout will want.

Most of us are familiar with the old story of the kid who, lacking proper tackle, ties a bent pin onto a length of kite string and proceeds to catch more fish than the adults around him. There's more than a smattering of truth here. Many country kids do catch fish on much less than sophisticated tackle. A willow branch, six feet of monofilament line, a small hook, and a few garden worms have been the undoing of countless trout. The kid catches trout in small brooks with such gear because he knows where the trout are likely to be and keeps a low profile as he lofts his worm into the hotspots. A rereading of the last chapter will give you some idea of where and how to dunk that worm.

WORM FISHING

In some pools, particularly if brook trout are present, a live garden worm will be seized the instant it touches the water. But not always. Larger trout and those that have been fished for frequently keep a close eye on what looks natural and what doesn't. It's always best to toss the worm upstream and above the best part of any pool and allow it to tumble along the bottom and

Moving cautiously along a small brook and tossing a live bait into likely looking spots is an excellent way to "learn" the water. Small trout are always hungry.

come into the trout's holding spot in a natural way. If the worm is jerked or pulled about in an unnatural way, it won't be considered by an experienced fish. (Perhaps trout can't learn in the human sense, but they sure know when things don't look right.)

When a fish grabs a worm, there's usually a bit of tug-tug-tugging on the line as it chews on the worm in order to render it easier to swallow. Following the tugging, a trout nearly always turns to swim to its hiding place to finish the swallowing. It does so to avoid having the worm taken away from it by another trout. As the fish begins to move away with the bait, you must set the hook with a smart jerk of the rod tip. If the stream is narrow and the trout less than a foot long, the best plan is to keep on pulling and drag the fish out, or air-lift it onto the bank. Such a

landing technique is not artistic—but it's effective.

Successful worm fishing can be done with a fly, spinning, or casting rod, and even with that historic willow branch. The size of the water will determine the best tackle. Small brooks and streams are best handled with a fly rod or spinning gear. Larger rivers and lakes can be better fished with spinning or casting gear. With casting tackle, however, you'll need a sinker, in addition to the worm, to cast properly. Spinning gear will toss a worm some distance without any weight.

A spinning or spincast reel attached to a fly rod is a great advantage when fishing a worm or other live bait. Using the long rod as a sort of pendulum, you can cast bait softly and accurately. With 6-pound-test monofilament, no leader is necessary—just tie a size 8 or 10 hook to the end of the line and go to it. The smooth mono slides through the guides easily and transmits the slightest nibble on the worm to the rod hand. If you want to fish flies, carry a fly reel loaded with a fly line.

Nearly every worm fishing specialist has a "secret way" of attaching the worm. Almost any system works as long as it allows both ends of the worm to wiggle so it looks alive. Replace any worm that appears dead or somewhat bedraggled.

There are times when weight is necessary in order to tumble the worm along the bottom. Don't use any if you can avoid it, and only add enough to create that natural appearance. In still water, too much weight will cause any fish to drop the bait quickly since it doesn't feel right.

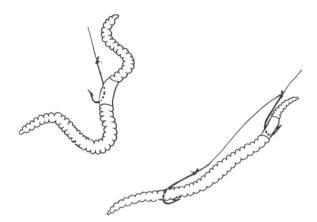

Garden worms are easy to find and very effective bait. On a single hook, allow both ends to dangle; trout usually find the movement irresistible. Two or more hooks tied together with monfilament, called a worm gang, are deadly with nightcrawlers.

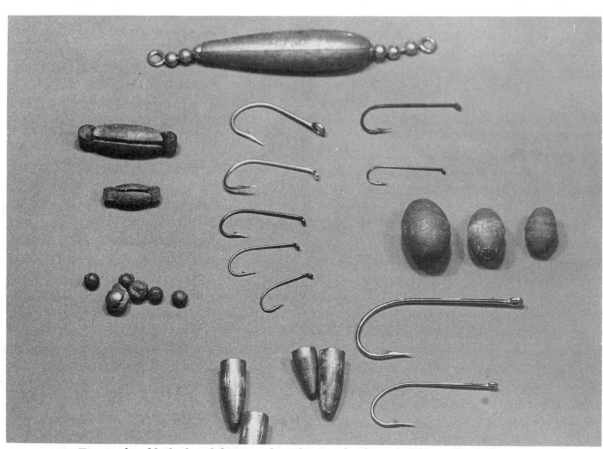

Terminal tackle for baitfishing can be as basic as hooks and sinkers. Shown here is a useful assortment of both.

When moving from one pool to another, where differing currents demand different amounts of weight, it's best to use sinkers that are easily removable. Split-shot sinkers are okay if they have those little "ears" that allow them to be pinched off and on. Twist-On sinkers work well and so do the rubber-cored type. The new "soft sinker" that is sold in paste form is also worth considering.

For trout in small brooks and ponds where fish aren't expected to reach trophy size, the best sort of worm is the little pink garden worm. These vary a bit in color but are generally pinkish gray. For larger fish, the red wiggler or night crawler is a better choice. All trout will grab both types of worms, but it's best to match the size of the worm to the size of trout expected.

Hooks for worm fishing should be chosen according to the size of worm used and size of fish expected. Sizes 6, 8, and 10 will cover most situations. Large night crawlers can be effectively fished with worm "gangs," which consist of two or more hooks on a single leader. This hooking arrangement is too deadly if any fish are to be released. The multiple hook points present an unhooking problem, especially if the worm is swallowed.

FISHING MINNOWS

A caution is required when choosing minnows as live bait. Some waters are off-limits to live minnows and others are restricted to kinds of minnows, so read your state or province regulations carefully. Many unwanted species have been accidentally introduced into some rivers. That said, it must be quickly added that live minnows are dynamite bait!

As with worms, the easiest way to fish a minnow is to hook one through the lips and toss it out. In lakes and still pools this is best done with the aid of a sinker that prevents the live minnow from swimming away from the desired spot. A neat way to accomplish this is to tie a blood knot in your mono line or leader, allowing one end of the excess material to extend from the knot about 12 inches.

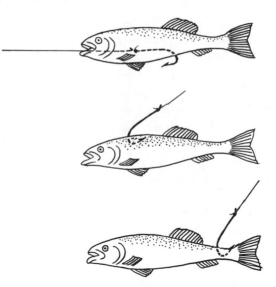

Three ways to hook a minnow. If the minnow is to be fished alive, the middle and bottom methods are recommended. The top method requires the use of a "minnow trace," a short section of twisted wire with a loop on each end, and is best for casting and retrieving the minnow.

This forms a "dropper." To this dropper attach the hook and to the extended end of the line or leader attach the sinker (see illustration). In some waters, you may find it helpful to attach a bobber above this arrangement in order to see if a customer is paying a visit.

When a trout grabs a minnow it usually does so with a rush, runs a short distance and then stops to turn the minnow so it can be swallowed head first. Wait for a solid pull before setting the hook. Strike too soon and you'll be minus a minnow.

The most effective method of minnow fishing in moving water is done with the help of a short wire "trace" and a split double hook. This involves sticking the wire into the minnow's mouth and thrusting it through the vent. The split hook is slipped through the loop in the wire and pulled into the body cavity (see illustration). Thus hooked, the minnow is cast just like a lure and retrieved in a series of jerks and minnowlike movements. It's a busy way to fish but highly effective if the trout are paying any attention that day.

GRASSHOPPERS AND CRICKETS

'Hoppers and crickets should be fished on the surface like a dry fly, without any weight. Use small hooks and try to attach them with the point thrust just under the "collar" so they remain alive. These land creatures are fun to fish with because the strikes are spectacular—even those of small trout. They really smack 'em!

I hesitate to reveal an old secret but I will if you promise not to tell anyone. If your grasshopper and cricket fishing is not going well, try attaching one to a size 10 hook with a dab of model cement. Hold the creature on the hook for a minute or so until it's stuck. Cast it into any pool containing trout and a quick strike is a sure thing.

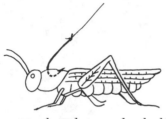

Grasshoppers and crickets are hooked by inserting the point just under the collar at the top of the thorax. If this is done carefully, the insect will be alive and kicking when it hits the water.

SALMON EGGS

Where rainbow trout and their western cousins are found, no other natural bait is as effective as real salmon eggs. A caution is in order, however, since genuine salmon eggs are forbidden by law on some waters and in some states. However, many excellent imitations are available that look and smell like the real thing, and they'll all catch fish if the angler does his job. And that doesn't mean merely tossing an egg-baited hook into the water.

Trout of the Pacific drainage system are attracted to salmon eggs because of their shared habitat with West Coast salmon. When a young rainbow, cutthroat, or Dolly Varden reaches a size large enough to swallow a whole salmon egg, it usually will grab every one it sees. Loose eggs that have escaped from a salmon nest come tumbling along the bottom at specific times of the year, not unlike a hatch of flies on other trout streams. Trout whose ancestors knew about salmon eggs never seem to lose their fondness for them. Properly presented, a salmon egg is as close to a guaranteed bait as any we know about.

A short-shank hook is the traditional choice for holding a salmon egg. The entire curve of the hook can be hidden inside the egg by inserting the point past the barb with a rolling motion. Only the eye of the hook is exposed. When hooked this way the egg can roll and tumble along the bottom in a natural manner, and because there is no hook point exposed, will seldom become snagged on rocks or flotsam. If possible, fish eggs without sinkers for a more natural appearance. If sinkers must be used pinch on only enough lead to keep the egg just ticking the bottom.

A trout usually gulps down an egg without hesitation. The solid tug-tug-tug is a sure signal you've got a fish on. A sharp jerk will easily drive the hook through the egg and into the fish. With imitation eggs or round pellets fashioned from gum drops or more dense materials it's usually wise to leave the tip of the hook exposed or nearly so. Trout won't hold the phoney baits as long as the real ones, so you'll have to strike quicker and with more authority.

OTHER BAITS

The widespread availability of stocked trout—that is, fish that have been reared in a hatchery—has occasioned the use of a number of baits that resemble the food pellets such trout eat while being raised. Whole kernel corn, cheese balls, small marshmallows, gum drops, and prepared pastes of many kinds are all possibilities. Rainbow trout in particular are attracted to such baits. These baits will all catch trout, and they are fished just like natural bait. Use single hooks in sizes 10, 8, or 6. Tip: These egglike baits are especially effective below dams in tailrace water.

7

Fishing with Lures

The basic method of fishing the average lure is to cast it some distance and then reel it back. The built-in action of spinning lures and swimming plugs does the job of enticing the fish—provided you cast that lure to a spot that holds a fish. Simple enough, right? The rub is, fish are not always precisely where they ought to be. Study the stream diagrams in Chapter 5 and try to fish the holding spots indicated, but if a trout doesn't hit, try different spots.

Casting a tiny lure into a shallow or extremely clear pool or lake can be done with finesse. Tossing a heavy spoon or other heavy lure into the same water may scare the daylights out of any fish that happens to be there. Select your lure with some thought given to the kind of water at hand. A good rule is to begin with a small lure and work up to larger ones if the fish don't pay any attention. Also, try lures of different colors and sizes.

No matter where you're fishing or with what, make the first few casts short ones. Fish the near water first and gradually extend your range until you've covered the water. If you're not familiar with the pool, you'll probably discover that some particular part of it is where the strikes will occur. If you see the flash of a fish or a disturbance on the surface that tells you a fish took a look but didn't take, try casting to the same spot again. If you keep on getting the same results—a flash or boil but no strike—try another lure. On any given day on any stream or lake, trout fall into what the bass fishermen call a "pattern." Once you discover the right lure and the right presentation, it's a safe bet you'll catch more than one.

In moving water, the current will add additional spin or wobble to most lures. For this reason, casting across and slightly downstream, then retrieving by cranking the reel handle will impart additional movement. At times, merely allowing the lure to drift with the current may impart enough action to bring a strike. But, if you do nothing except cast and reel your victories will be limited. Like people, I think fish can become bored with the same old thing. Some extra jerks, delays, and change of retrieving speeds can work wonders.

One of the best variations that can be added to a retrieve is a quick change of speed, shifting gears from fast to slow and vice versa. I prefer a three-stage speed-up because I think it more closely suggests how a baitfish acts when it senses danger is approaching. As the lure strikes the water, allow it to sink freely for about ten or twelve inches. Then begin to move it slowly. If it's a spinning lure, the blade should rotate at a slow "waltz" speed. Bring it along for about six or eight feet and then shift into slightly higher speed causing the blade to rotate twice as fast. Another six or eight feet of this, and then really begin to crank—so fast that the spinning blade becomes a blur. This trick works much better for me than a stop-and-start routine, which, by the way, is a highly recommended bass fishing technique.

Stop-and-start retrieving and trolling *will* produce in lakes and ponds when trout are the target fish because of the lack of escape cover in open water. When a trout sets its sights on a minnow in a lake, the minnow can only do one thing and that's swim fast—for its life. If it begins to lose the race, the only other alternatives are to change speed or direction. You can suggest this by raising or lowering the rod tip and switching it from side to side, changing reel speed at the same time. Modern high-speed reels make this easy to do from a mechanical standpoint. What you must do is mix and match your rod action and retrieving speed in ways that suggest a fleeing baitfish. Trying different routines is fun in itself, and when you hit one that works, hang on. The strike to a fast-moving lure can be jarring!

There will be more tips and information about fishing with lures in other chapters, but about here is a good place to talk about how to attach lures to our lines. Many spinning lures have a tendency to twist line after a short period of casting and retrieving no matter what knot is used. Many anglers avoid this problem by using swap swivels next to the lure. These keep the line free of twists and allow quick lure changing. The fish don't seem to mind the extra hardware most of the time, but if you think it matters, an alternate system is to use a small barrel swivel about a foot away from the lure. This will also prevent line twist and allow use of an improved clinch knot at the lure. For trolling lures a barrel *and* a snap-swivel can be used for additional protection against line twist.

SELECTING LURES

Even a casual reader will have noticed, by this time, that fishing for trout is a sport full of maybes, almosts, frequentlys, and sometimes. It is, because there are so many variables in angling that many techniques can work on a given day—and often do. That's the reason there are so many lure shapes, sizes, and colors. It's true that some anglers do well with a handful of lures, and it's also true that some highly accomplished ones limit themselves to a single lure—at least they say they do. But it's a lot more fun to try new lures and develop a few favorites of your own.

Lures with Blades

A good group of lures to begin with are those with rotating blades. A dozen or more manufacturers offer proven ones, and it's a safe bet that more trout are caught on them than any other type of lure. These lures have a metal blade that rotates around a wire shaft. The spinning blade picks up reflections from the available light and the water and suggests a swimming baitfish. A piece of metal or plastic attached to the shaft adds another color, and the hook, usually a small treble (three pointed), may be adorned with feathers, squirrel-tail hair, or synthetic material. These components can add up to uncountable color variations, making the choices wide indeed.

Is there a best color? Probably not, but there are some proven colors and metallic finishes that deserve a place in any tacklebox.

Silver gets the nod as the all-time favorite among experienced anglers. A flashing silver spinner blade will attract trout and salmon more often than any other color. This is probably due to the metallic sheen on the sides of many baitfish. Brass, copper, and gold do the same, but these colors don't appear to be as bright as silver

An assortment of spinning lures. The flashing, revolving blade suggests a swimming baitfish. Some spinning lures are dressed with feathers, hair, or even a plastic minnow.

in clear water. But we have a bit of a puzzle here, because the yellowish metals do seem to be more visible in cloudy or discolored water. Thus, if the water isn't very clear, and silver lures are not producing, switch to gold, brass, or copper. The same applies to lures other than spinners.

Other colors, those of the shaft or skirt of the lure, introduce a whole new set of options. It's never a mistake to have a touch of red on any lure. It's the color of blood, and no matter how the idea strikes you, game fish are predators and are attracted to it. Red can, however, be emphasized too much. On metallic lures it seems that just a hint of red is much better than a big patch of it.

When rainbow trout and the sea-run rainbows (steelheads) are the fish sought, red, orange, and yellow are always colors to consider. They are because rainbow trout are not adverse to eating the eggs of other rainbow trout and these colors suggest them. A silver blade over a red plastic bead or a spinning lure with a red or orange tail is a frequent first choice on a rainbow river.

Not many years ago, the use of blue or green on any sort of lure was not popular. It was common wisdom that since few natural creatures were blue or green, using such colors was not worth the effort. Extensive tests conducted by divers and researchers in underwater tanks proved that blue held its color even at great depths. Greenish-blues did too, whereas reds, oranges, and yellows tended to fade out in deep water. Today, blue and green lures are quite popular; we even have metallic "colors" that blend these tones with silver for a most attractive combination.

Spoons

Next in popularity to the rotating-blade lures are the ones known as spoons. These are slabs of metal showing a slight curve in their profiles that cause them to wobble back and forth, or shimmy, as they're retrieved or trolled. Again, the idea is to suggest a baitfish, and spoons do it well. Spoons are made in sizes as small as one inch long to whoppers the size of a banana, and all of them can be put to good use. The size of the fish and depth of the water being fished are the regulating factors. Use the big ones for deep trolling for trout in lakes and the small ones for stream trout.

Swimming Lures

Plugs are the third most important group of lures for trout and salmon and offer the widest variety of shapes and colors. You describe it and there's probably a lure that looks like anything one could dream up. Basically, however, they are all torpedo-shaped, since that's what small fish look like. A good rule of thumb is to have some lures in your box that are similar in appearance to the baitfish that inhabit the lake or stream you happen to be fishing. This isn't as complicated as it seems, because nearly all baitfish are dark on their backs and white on their bellies. A few lures that are black and brown, or dark green or blue

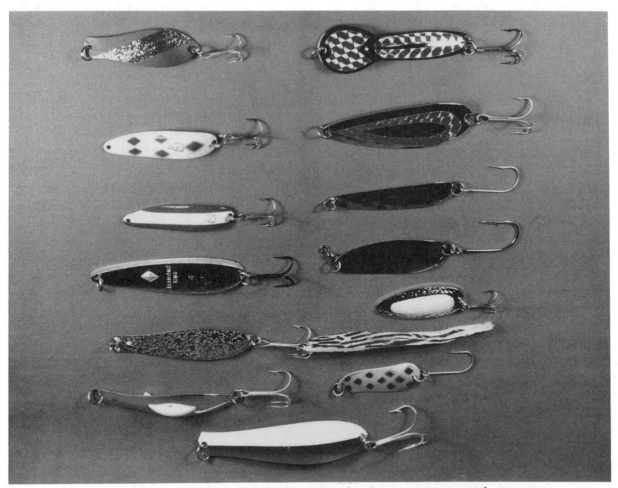

Spoons are designed to wobble from side to side. If a spoon rotates in the water, the line will become twisted and eventually tangled. Best way to avoid this is to use a snap swivel.

A selection of smaller lures that are suitable for casting or trolling with spinning tackle. The addition of a painted eye seems to be attractive to trout and salmon.

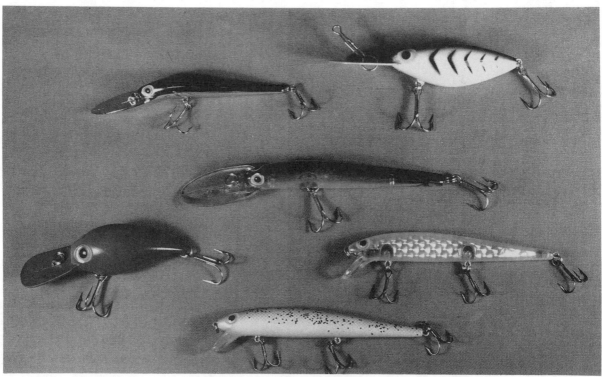

Lures that are designed to dive when trolled or retrieved are identified by the longer lip in front. You'll know when they're working right—you'll feel a tug-tug on the rod handle as they swim.

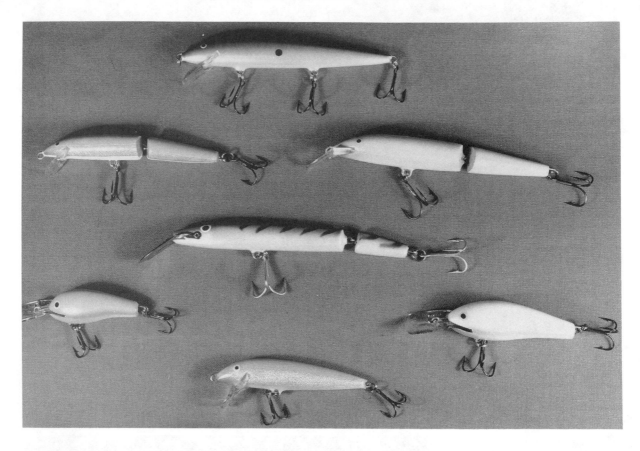

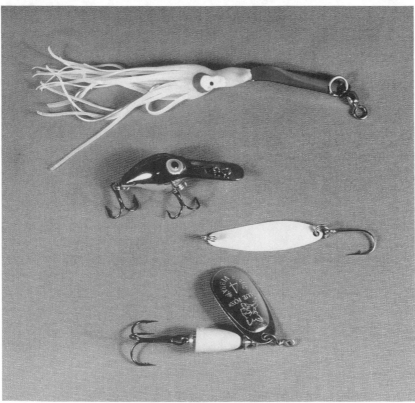

Another assortment of swimming minnow lures including a couple of jointed models. There are days when the extra wiggle provided by the joint is the magic touch.

Fishing lures do not always resemble something we think a fish would like. These lures have all proven to be excellent steelhead producers on the West Coast, as well as brown trout catchers in the Great Lakes.

Large minnow-type lure fooled this big lake trout into believing it was indeed a minnow. Such look-alike lures are universal favorites, but sometimes fish will go for lures that look like nothing under the sun.

on the top side, and white or silver on the bottom, will suggest most small minnows. At times some showing a dash of red or orange will do well and so will an all-black one. The latter can be especially good if there are small catfish in the water.

Regardless of where you're fishing, the most useful lure sizes will be in the range of 2 to 3½ inches. This is trout size, and lures in this range will catch fish 90 percent of the time. Spend some time talking to the local angling talent for tips on preferred colors and sizes and the best techniques for using them. If everyone on the water is catching trout on a black-and-red Mepps or a Brown-trout Rebel that happens to be 2½ inches long, you'd be well advised to try it.

8

Fly Fishing

In recent years, fly fishing, especially for trout, has become increasingly popular. Anglers and would-be anglers of all ages and both genders have discovered that fly fishing for trout is fun, productive, and as basic or complicated as one chooses to make it. It's also not as expensive as most people believe.

A lot of words have been written by well-meaning angler/journalists insisting that fly fishing is not difficult to learn. At the same time, an equally large number of articles and books have been published that are quite detailed and complex, leading neophytes to believe that fly fishing is difficult and perhaps well beyond their capabilities. As with many recreational activities, the truth lies between these extremes. Anyone with somewhat above room temperature IQ can learn the *basics of fly casting* with a few hours of instruction and practice. The beginner can also grasp the *fundamentals* of fly selection and other rudiments in less than a day or so on the water. He or she will not become a *highly skilled* fly angler in a week or a year or perhaps several

years. To reach the upper levels of the sport requires many years of practice and observation. But trust me; if you find it's fun after a try or two, I'll bet you continue the learning process and advance quickly. I know of no other form of fishing that's more fun, more thought provoking, or wears better as a lifetime sport.

LEARNING TO FLY CAST

At this point, it's hoped that you've acquired that all-round 8- or 8½-foot fly rod marked for a 6-weight line. It's also assumed that you've attached a leader to that line of the length and taper suggested in the section on leaders. For practice, select any old fly and cut off the point of the hook with wire cutters. Pull twenty feet of line and leader from the reel and stretch it out in front of you on the lawn or nearby vacant lot. Holding the rod firmly (but not in a death grip) bring it up smartly from a horizontal to just behind vertical. This is known as the "1 o'clock position," the perfectly vertical being 12 o'clock. If this is done with some quickness, the line and leader will rise up and float back over your shoulder and straighten out behind you. As the line reaches full extension, you'll feel a slight tug on the rod tip. That's the signal to bring the rod forward to the 10 o'clock position and allow the line to straighten out in front. All the while, you should be holding the line between the reel and the first guide with your noncasting hand. This hand is important in fly casting, because you'll feel the tugs as the line straightens in front and behind, signaling you when to move the rod.

By scribing a long oval in the air with the rod tip, you can make the line move back and forth smoothly without any visible jerks or excess hesitation. Eventually, every fly caster develops a style of his or her own, but at first, this oval technique is quite easy to master. If it doesn't feel smooth, stop the backcast a bit sooner or later, until the line flows forward and backward in even loops.

The back and forth movements are called "false casting." False casting serves a practical fishing purpose when using dry flies. It shakes the excess water from the fly, line, and leader allowing them to land in a relatively dry condition.

After three or four false casts—from 10 o'clock to 1 o'clock—allow the line and leader to fall to the grass, as you release the excess line in the other hand. If the fly drops to the imaginary spot you had in mind, or close to it, you've made great progress. If it doesn't, try changing the timing one way or the other. It's not unlike riding a bicycle; once you've got the idea imprinted on the brain and casting arm, it won't be forgotten easily. You'll know when you're doing it right.

Extending the cast requires more line to be carried in the air and a slightly longer wait for the back cast to straighten. If you come forward too soon, the line will wrap around the tip of the rod or your neck or fall down in heap.

Remember, when you're false casting the line

His line unfurling behind him in a graceful backcast, the author waits for it to reach full extension. Note how the rod is angled slightly to the right on the backcast; half of the oval that prevents the line from hitting it.

BASIC OVERHEAD CAST

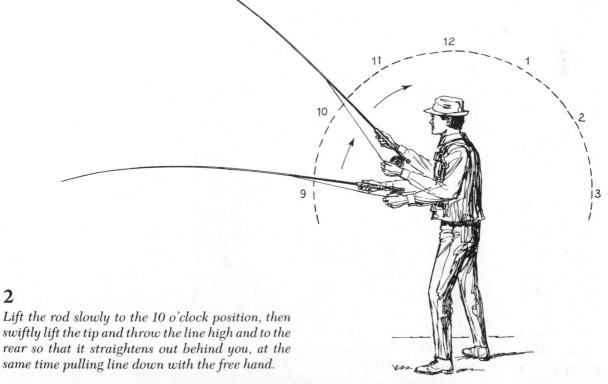

1

With about twenty feet of line extended in front of you on a lawn or vacant lot, grasp the line in your free hand. Hold the rod firmly, with the thumb on top to give added support.

2

Lift the rod slowly to the 10 o'clock position, then swiftly lift the tip and throw the line high and to the rear so that it straightens out behind you, at the same time pulling line down with the free hand.

STEP 3 ➜

3

Stop the backcast at 1 o'clock, and turn slightly to see if the line is extended behind you and not dropping too low.

4

As the line reaches full extension, and you feel a tug, pause for an instant, then start the forward cast, scribing a slight oval in the air with the rod tip.

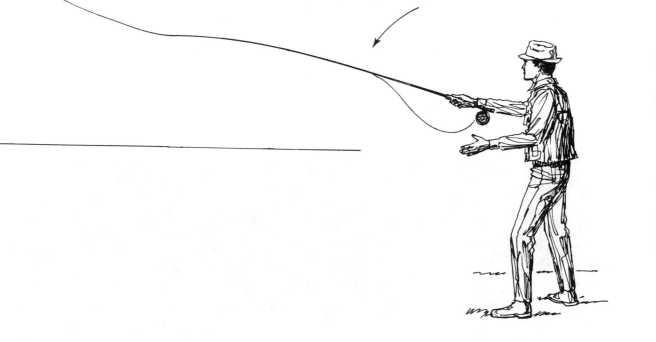

5

The line should come forward in a tight loop and straighten out in front of you. Stop the rod at about 10 o'clock, aiming the fly at a point about three feet above the ground, and release the line held in the left hand. Line will shoot through the guides and settle to the ground as you lower the rod. After you've mastered this basic backcast and forward cast, practice false casting—that is, keeping the line in the air a few times—as described in the text.

Here the line is at full extension on the backcast, and the author is about to begin his forward cast. Note how his left hand pulls down on the line for added power.

The forward cast at the point of maximum power. Again, note angler's left hand pulling down on the line to give added flex to the rod and more power to the cast.

must be moving at all times in order to stay aloft. Rod action accomplishes this and, of course, you must keep the rod moving. At first, this will be a little tiring if you stay at it for sustained periods. Take a break. Enjoy the learning process and let the rod do the work instead of trying to force the line with brute strength.

Fly casting is a game of timing not muscle power. The most frail of adults and children of five or six, are capable of casting a fly line seventy-five feet or more without breaking a sweat.

The Roll Cast

The direct overhead cast is the best way to present a fly most of the time. Some trouble arises when a high bank, trees, or brush behind you interfere with your backcast. Learning the roll cast on grass is impossible, because water is needed to make it work. It's the surface tension of the water applied to the line that brings this seemingly impossible trick together.

It's called a roll cast because the line "rolls" in a wide circle, thus propelling the leader and fly in a kind of loop-the-loop manner. Begin by pulling the line across the water with the rod by raising the rod tip towards vertical. As the rod reaches a point about six inches *past* vertical, snap the wrist forward, stopping the rod just before it reaches horizontal. The line and leader will scoot across the surface toward you and then unfurl in the opposite direction. Sound difficult? Well, it may be the first time or two you try it, but it's really quite easy if you remember one tip: *never* allow the line to lose contact with the water. Some line *must* touch the water for the roll cast to work its magic.

What you've just read constitutes the foundation of fly casting. There are many other subtleties that you'll learn as time passes. Another complete book could be written on casting alone—and several have been. By studying the illustrations and practicing as often as possible, the movements and theory of fly casting should come easy to most beginners.

I must admit that the best instruction I ever received was gained by watching others. An hour spent observing a good fly caster is worth all the instruction books in the world. If you have a friend who fly fishes, don't be shy about asking for some hands-on instruction. If approached with a wistful look, there are few accomplished anglers who won't be flattered at being asked. And that's another nice thing about fly fishing; the sport seems to have a mellowing effect on all who become involved with it. Sharing information and helping newcomers are part of the sport. Everyone was once a beginner, and most veterans remember that they too needed some help at the outset.

If you enjoy being involved with groups, various companies and clubs offer fly fishing schools that include casting instruction, courses in fly and tackle selection, entomology, and on-stream lessons. The Orvis Company, Fenwick, and several other tackle makers sponsor such classes as do dozens of local tackle shops and organizations. Check fishing magazines and ask your tackle shop about such schools. Schools are usually conducted on weekends. Most novices find it more comfortable to learn with others who are at the same level.

FISHING THE DRY FLY

The dry fly is the most fun for new anglers because the strikes take place on the surface of the water where the action can be seen. It remains the favorite method of many experienced anglers for the same reason. There's a curious paradox here, however, because dry-fly fishing can be quite easy on certain days and totally frustrating the next. For a number of reasons, most of which are known only to the trout, nearly any dry fly will catch fish on Monday and not do so on Tuesday. This is one of the many mysteries that makes fly fishing the fascinating sport that it is.

The perfect scenario for dry-fly fishing is to be on the water when a hatch of mayflies is rising up from the bottom to be transformed from the nymphal stage to winged adults. These mayflies exist in hundreds of species and subspecies and

ROLL CAST

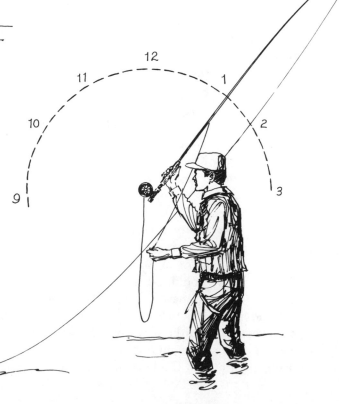

1

With about twenty feet of line on the water in front of you, slowly raise the rod, angled away from your body, so the line slides along the water toward you.

2

Stop the rod at about 1 o'clock. The line should fall from the rod tip as shown.

3

Pause for an instant at 1 o'clock, then snap the rod forward sharply. The line will roll over and straighten out, then drop gently to the water.

This is a mayfly, the insect that most dry flies try to imitate. These creatures come in a variety of colors and sizes, and there are an equal number of artificials available to match them.

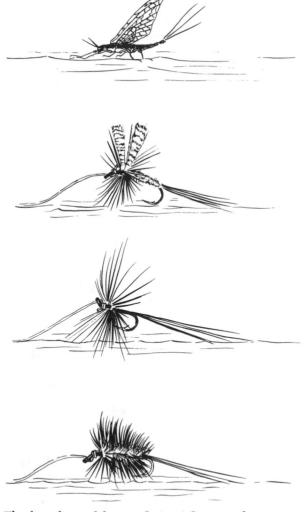

The dun phase of the mayfly (top) floats on the water at emergence. Three types of dry flies that try to suggest it are the featherwing, spider, and bivisible.

come in assorted sizes and colors. Different species hatch at different times of the year. Add to the mayflies the other forms of aquatic insects such as stoneflies, caddisflies, and craneflies, toss in another hundred land-born insects and the need for a wide variety of artificial flies becomes apparent. Even the most complete of anglers doesn't carry a fly to suggest every insect he may encounter, but he does have a selection that can generally cover the spectrum.

Dry Flies to Start With

Adams—sizes 10, 12, 14, 16, 18
Light Cahill—same sizes as above
Gordon Quill—same sizes as above
Grey Hackle Peacock—14, 16, 18
Royal Wulff—10, 12, 14
Olive Dun—14, 16, 18, 20
Badger Bivisible—10, 12, 14
Black Beetle—12, 14, 16
Brown Ant 14, 16, 18
Grasshopper—pick one that suggests the local 'hopper size and colors, 10, 12 and 14

If you examine these fly patterns you'll see that the somber hues of most natural mayflies are covered. Browns, grays, bluish/grays (the *dun* colors), light tan and olive predominate. Few natural mayflies or other insects trout prefer are vividly colored. The most flamboyant of the pat-

A typical spider dry fly. Spiders are wonderful flies for coaxing a strike when few natural flies are present. When given movement, they resemble a fluttering insect.

Terrestrials are tiny flies that imitate land insects. They're great trout catchers on nearly all streams. Fishing them requires fine-diameter leaders and a soft hand on the rod to avoid break-offs.

terns listed is the Royal Wulff. The white hair-wings of this pattern are easy to see on the water and it does well when the more conservative flies don't produce. There are many other patterns which will do as well as the ones listed because they are of the same general size and color. In every locale there are favorites and every angler has his own special flies. Pay attention to the local talent!

Tactics

If a good hatch is in progress, take a moment to watch what's going on before making a fly selection. Try to catch one of the hatching insects. Study it and tie on an imitation that comes close to matching it in size and color. While color is important, size is probably more so. If you tie on a fly the size of a hummingbird and the natural insects the trout are feeding on are less than a half inch long, your success will be limited.

When you see a fish rise, creating a well-defined splash or ring on the surface as it grabs a natural, get into position to make your first cast. If possible, that position should be slightly behind and to one side of the fish. Aim the cast to drop about four feet upstream from where the rise was and allow the fly to float over that spot. Don't wiggle or jiggle the fly or jerk the rod. The presentation you're trying for is a free-floating insect that looks like an easy bite to the feeding trout.

If the trout rises to snatch your fly from the surface, it may do so with a rush and a splash. Set the hook by raising the rod tip as the fly vanishes in the splash, and if the fishing gods are smiling, you'll have your first fish caught on a dry fly. If you don't hook it try again. The trout, especially if it's larger than average, may suck the fly in gently without making much surface disturbance. Keep your eye on the fly. If it disappears in the tiniest of wakes, strike with a positive but not violent movement. Yes, I know that sounds like a difficult thing to do in the excitement of the moment, but in time it can be done. Even the best of anglers goof-up on strikes more often than they'll admit to, so don't be too critical of yourself.

If you see a trout or two come to your fly and refuse it, or strike "short," it's a good indication that the fly is too large. Wait a few minutes and try a smaller one. If that doesn't work, switch to a different pattern. If trout are feeding regularly, you can usually seduce some of them by experimenting with colors and sizes.

When you find yourself on a stream that seems devoid of insect life at the moment, a good approach is to try an attractor pattern such as the Royal Wulff, a bivisible, grasshopper imitation, or beetle. With such dry flies, when there are no rises, "fishing the water" instead of "fishing the rise" is called for. A quick look at the pool dia-grams in Chapter 5 will show you the likely spots to try. This is "confidence" fishing. Cast the fly above and slightly beyond the places you think a trout ought to be and allow the fly to drift freely. Don't give up after a cast or two. Try at least ten casts, repeat the process after moving a step or two. Really cover the water. Not every trout that spies your fly will take it, but persistence pays off on most days if the fish are not too spooky.

In other situations, a hatch of caddisflies could put trout into a feeding frenzy and the dead drift method may not work. If you see insects scooting and scurrying about and some reckless splashing, it's time to do some scooting of your own. Cast the fly near the last splash, and as soon as it lands, twitch the rod tip and pull the excess line with the noncasting hand, and move the fly across the surface. Sometimes strikes to such a "worked" fly will scare the bejabbers out of anyone—beginner and old hand alike. These strikes occur with lightning speed and may catch you off guard. Trout taking a moving fly are amazingly good marksmen and often end up hooking themselves. All that's needed is a slight twist of the wrist and you've got him. Your reaction should be quick but not hard.

When it's necessary to turn to small flies, that is, those size 16 and smaller, that "twist of the wrist" becomes very important. With such a tiny hook, and an even smaller barb, a movement of a quarter-inch is all that's needed to accomplish hooking. Trout take such tiny flies slowly and positively, and to strike too quickly or too severely will pull the little hook between their lips without penetrating. Try for a slow *pull* instead of a sharp jab.

Playing and Landing Your Trout

The trout has taken your fly, and now a different set of skills comes into play. The index finger of the hand holding the rod should be crooked around the line. The line is held loosely as the fly is drifting downstream, and slack line is stripped in under the finger. As the strike occurs, the index finger pinches down the line, holding it tightly against the grip. If the fish runs immediately, the hand holding loose line must allow it to pay out under the index finger of the rod hand. It sounds like a lot of things are happening at once, and they are, but a glance at the illustration will show what we're talking about.

You'll note that pinching the line with your index finger as slack line is cranked back onto the reel requires that a right-handed person reel with the left hand. Curiously, the majority of right-handed fly anglers do not do this. They transfer the rod from right to left hand and crank with their right hand. I'm in a minority here, but I strongly urge all beginners to learn to fish with their *smart* hand, be it right or left and reel with the opposite. All quality reels can be adjusted so the handle is on either the right or left side. Switching hands has lost many big fish. Handling

slack line with the left hand and then changing hands to reel it in has never made sense to me. Spinning reels are cranked with the "dumb" hand, so why can't fly reels?

Try to retrieve loose line as soon as possible. With the line still pinched between finger and grip, reel up the vagrant coils quickly and evenly. This is called "getting the fish on the reel." It's a good habit to acquire. If the big fish of your dreams is hooked, it's much easier to play it from the reel instead of keeping track of the slack line that's between your legs, around your neck, or elsewhere.

Small trout can be handled without getting the slack back on the reel, but any trout larger than a pound or so can create strange problems.

If your reel has been adjusted so the handle is on the left side, all you have to do when a fish strikes is clip the line against the rod with your fingers (left), reel in slack, and play the fish from the reel (right). If your handle is on the right side, play a small fish by stripping in line with the left hand, a large one by changing hands and reeling with your right.

A two-footer can create havoc. Getting fish "on the reel" applies to all forms of fly fishing. A fly reel with a slick drag can release line in a much smoother manner than your wet, nervous fingers. As the fish runs, allow the reel handle to turn freely; as the fish tires, reel up the excess. Nothing to it!

WET-FLY FISHING

Wet flies may be the forgotten member of the fly fishing family on some waters due to the popularity of dry flies and the more recent nymphs. When anglers of today are not casting dry flies they're probably using nymphs, which are designed to suggest the juvenile forms of aquatic insects. The distinction between nymphs and wet flies is a fuzzy one to most anglers regardless of their experience (the author included). Traditional wet flies are basically versions of dry flies tied sparsely to allow them to sink instead of

A wet fly (top) and three types of nymphs. Both wets and nymphs imitate mayflies in one or another of their subsurface forms.

The Gold-Ribbed Hare's Ear, a typical wet fly, is one of the most effective of all patterns. It has caught trout the world over.

float. The idea is to suggest an insect on its way to the surface, where it will hatch into an adult.

In practice, wet flies can be jiggled and jerked, allowed to drift free or swing with the current. Trout may take them to be hatching insects, small minnows, or heaven knows what else. At any rate, wet flies have been catching trout for several centuries whereas dry flies and the more sophisticated nymphs are comparatively recent arrivals.

It can be argued that conventional wet flies and nymphs serve the same purpose, but there are times one will catch fish with regularity and the other won't. Find a fly fisherman with plenty of patches on his boots and you'll usually find a wet-fly advocate. In my opinion, downstream wet-fly fishing remains the most effective way of catching trout that's been discovered.

What we have in discussing the best and easiest fly fishing method for a beginner to lead off with is a kind of "chicken and egg" situation. In watching dozens of budding anglers take to the trout stream for the first time, I've noticed that most of them prefer starting with the dry fly. They seem to like it because they can see the fly right there on top, and if a trout grabs it the action is quite evident. They also know if the fly is "dragging" and how currents can alter its drift. Because the fly is floating, they also know when their cast is close to a rising fish.

While I strongly believe that trout are easier to catch on wet flies when they are cast across and downstream, beginners don't seem to react as quickly to a strike when they can't see the fly. In addition, their eyes and reflexes are not yet well enough honed to read the subtle "winks and flashes" that take place underwater when trout

are striking in a less than positive manner. Dry-fly casting can also teach a novice a great deal about wet-fly fishing. As a dry fly reaches its maximum downstream swing and sinks, a trout often strikes it. This may be because the movement of the fly finally provokes the trout to strike. The dry fly is actually being fished "wet" at the end of the cast. Such hook-ups are often accidents—and thank goodness for them. But the technique can be employed purposely—with excellent results. This is particularly true when emerging mayflies are plentiful.

Casting a wet fly (or flies, if droppers are used) slightly across and downstream is the best way to begin. The current will move the flies at a steady pace and frequently this alone will bring a strike. This is referred to as a "dead drift."

When the simple downstream drift doesn't bring a strike, try jiggling the rod tip. When fluttering caddisflies or stoneflies are on the surface, violently jerking the fly often provokes a

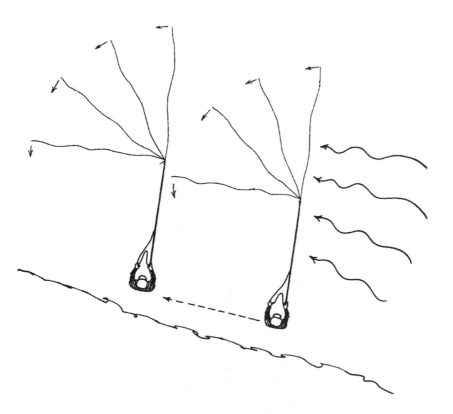

Casting wet flies across and slightly downstream is an easy and rewarding method. Cast the fly, let the current sweep it downstream, and then retrieve it by stripping line in short jerks. Then wade a few feet downstream and repeat the procedure. Note: In actuality, line would be much longer than shown in this diagram.

Retrieving line in short strokes can be done by the hand-twist method (above). The line is brought into the palm with the fingers. On the next cast, it will jump out of the hand as the line shoots through the guides (right).

strike. Watch what the naturals do and try to duplicate their actions. Movement can also be applied to your fly by stripping the line in jerks as it drifts, creating a stop-start-stop cadence. A wet fly can be retrieved by what is known as the "hand-twist" method (see illustration). When flies are retrieved in this manner it imparts a throbbing, lifelike action. All of these retrieving methods can be mixed on the same cast or varied from one cast to the next.

As you gain experience, special movements and tricks will become part of *your* style. If you mentally catalog or write down what worked on a given day in an angling diary, you'll be able to repeat the performance another time. After a couple of seasons, applying past experience becomes automatic, and you'll be well on your way to becoming an accomplished angler.

In order to extend the distance a free-drifting wet fly or floating dry will travel, before the current bellies the line and drags the fly unnaturally through the water, it's necessary to "mend" the line without lifting the fly from the water. This involves picking up some but not all of the line and, once it's in the air, flipping the rod smartly and tossing the line upstream, as shown in the accompanying drawing.

Fishing More Than One Fly

Downstream wet-fly fishing is usually more productive when two or three flies are cast on the same leader, instead of a single fly as is common in other forms of fly fishing. Fishing a pair or trio of wet flies at the same time can lead to complicated tangles, but shouldn't if casts are made slowly and the leader is constructed properly.

The best leader for wet flies is the same one used for dry flies, with one exception. It has "droppers" to accommodate the extra flies. A dropper can be made by extending one of the blood knots that connect different diameters of monofilament as the tapered leader is being constructed (see drawing). Plan the leader in such a way that the droppers are at least twenty inches apart. If the extra flies are that far apart there is less chance of them tangling. They can be spaced as much as three feet if you're using only two. More than three can be used, but the problems associated with this are many and not worth the extra knots. You can also tie a dropper to a knotted leader with a clinch knot (see drawing).

The most compelling reason for using a multiple fly rig is the effect it has on a curious trout. A

8-17
Mending the line. To prolong the natural drift of a fly when the current begins to belly the line, lift the bellied part from the water and flip it back upstream.

Dropper for second fly can be made by extending one strand of the blood knot that joins two strands of a leader.

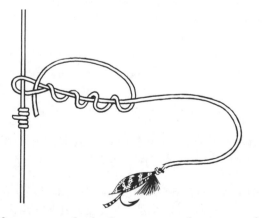

Alternate method of tying in a dropper with an improved clinch knot.

single fly drifting naturally or being retrieved may coax a strike if there are a lot of real insects present. When natural food is scarce, the sight of two or three little bugs drifting by is a greater enticement. Then too, there is the obvious advantage of offering the trout three different choices. With experience, you'll discover that one particular fly on a three-fly rig will often be the "fly of the day" and gather most of the strikes. At other times, the pattern may not be the deciding factor but the position on the leader will. If three flies are allowed to drift, three different depths are being exposed.

When mayflies are hatching in abundance, you'll notice that most strikes tend to occur just as the artificials reach the maximum point of swing in the current and begin to rise towards the surface. The pull of the rod and the force of the current bring the flies to the surface, simulating the movement of natural insects. This is another reason why downstream wet-fly fishing is effective and relatively easy.

The Self-Hooking Rod

When wet flies are nearly straight below us in the current, many fish will hook themselves as they seize the fly and turn toward their holding spot. A much higher percentage of wet-fly strikes will result in hooked fish if the rod has a "slow" action. A high percentage of modern fly rods are designed for dry-fly fishing, which requires a lot of false casting as well as long, accurate casts. As a result, such shafts are quite stiff and snap back from the force of a strike, pulling the fly from the fish's mouth before it's hooked. A perfect rod for wet-fly fishing should bend quite easily at the tip and be what the old timers used to call a "self-hooker."

In years gone by, all fly rods were of this "soft" persuasion. They resembled buggy whips, and they didn't cast a fly very far. But they sure did hook fish on short downstream casts with two or more wet flies.

Quick dry-fly rods are fine casting instruments, but they don't do that well with wet flies. Fortunately, there's an easy way to remedy this: use a line that's a size or two heavier than the one the rod maker recommends.

Using a heavier line for downstream wet fly fishing transforms some stiff rods into "self-hookers" because the extra weight forces the rod to bend more, thus slowing its recovery speed. A fish grabbing a wet fly that is stationary or being pulled against the current can swim some distance *before* feeling the hook point. By then, it's hooked itself!

This soft-action business is one of the reasons some experienced anglers continue to fish with vintage bamboo rods. They are more resilient and give when you hook a trout on a very light leader. Besides, there's the romance (and a spot of snobbishness) of fishing with a hand-crafted bamboo rod.

While the 6-weight line has been touted heavily as being the ideal trout weight, don't hesitate to use a 7-weight if it casts better for wet or dry flies. Similarly, if a rod rated for a 4- or 5-weight line casts a 6-weight better or easier go for it. Most beginners and not a few practiced hands will cast more comfortably and accurately with a line that's just a trifle heavy for their rod.

Wet Flies to Start With

As with dry flies, every experienced angler has a personal list of favorites. I'm no exception. Duplicating the basic insect colors is more important with wet flies than with dries because the fly is beneath the surface where the fish can see it all, in detail. The following list of wet flies will cover most situations nationwide.

Gold-Ribbed Hare's Ear: This fly is the best all-round wet fly ever created. It appears on every significant list. It's a scruffy, scraggly looking grayish-brown creation that suggests a multitude of aquatic creatures. *If I could have but one wet fly this would be it.*

Leadwing Coachman: Almost as useful as the Hare's Ear, the great attraction of the LW Coachman comes from its peacock herl body, an iridescent material that cannot be duplicated.

Gordon Quill: Another traditional pattern that suggests a host of dun-gray insects. (Avoid the Gordon Quills that favor a "bluish" cast; neutral gray is better).

Light Cahill: An excellent pattern that covers the late spring and summer mayflies in cream-ish shades. (Many commercial flies in this pattern are too brownish—stick with the light shades.)

Professor: This is a flashy "attractor" pattern with a red tail, yellow body, and gold ribbing. It will often interest trout when the more somber colors don't produce. An excellent producer on rainbow trout.

Royal Coachman: This old favorite doesn't resemble any insect common to trout streams yet its white wing and peacock-and-red body have been a winning combination for well over a century. Always have some RCs in the fly box.

Black Gnat: You'll need a black fly of some sort and the Gnat is as good as any.

Most useful sizes for all are 16, 14, 12, and 10.

Wet-fly patterns can be counted in the hundreds, perhaps thousands, if we include the regional "specials" and odd creations tied by experimentally inclined anglers. There are plenty of patterns that can be substituted for the half dozen I've suggested. As with dry flies, the browns, grays, creams, and blacks are the natural shades needed, with a bright, flashy pattern or two rounding out the initial selection.

As you fish more, you'll discover new patterns that may suit you better. Everyone does. The important thing to remember is that pattern alone will seldom make up for *presentation*, which is simply a buzz word for fishing skill. Having some idea of *where* to cast the fly, at the right time, will help create that wonderful thing known as "fisherman's luck."

NYMPH FISHING

The word nymph refers to the stage of an aquatic insect's life just prior to its becoming a winged adult. There are other underwater creatures which do not grow to become winged flies, such as scuds, creepers, and the like, but they too are generally termed nymphs in the angler's vernacular. Standard wet flies do a fair job of suggesting many nymph forms, but the flies tied in a more lifelike manner do it better. Such flies are designed to sink quickly and be fished on or near the bottom.

A few nymphs are tied on light wire hooks and are dressed sparsely in such a way that they float on or near the surface film. They are often called "emergers," because that's what their natural counterparts are—they're emerging from their nymphal shuck to become adult insects. Both sorts of nymphs will be useful at times, but the deeply fished nymphs are much more important, chiefly because trout eat more of them. Some anglers insist that underwater nymphs are the trouts' most important food source. That's undoubtedly true in some waters that are rich in insect variety.

Here is a good time to insert an observation concerning the volume of entomology an angler needs to know. With close to a half century of fly fishing for trout now behind me, I'm quite sure that memorizing the Latin names for insects trout feed on adds little to one's angling ability. It can be great fun if learning such things adds to your overall pleasure. Becoming a good observer on the stream and being able to determine size and color of the available insects is important. Some of the finest anglers I've fished with wouldn't know *Stenonema vicarium* from *Hexagenia limbata*. They *would know* that there are two brownish flies with one being larger than the other. That's enough to know to select the right fly. If insect taxonomy interests you, study the subject to your heart's content. The avenues of fly fishing pleasure are many.

Fishing the Deep Nymph

Since we left you hanging back there with the observation that trout eat a lot of nymphs on or near the bottom, we'll now explain how to fish the artificials. When there is no surface activity and traditional wet flies don't seem to bring much action, it's a good bet that a drifting nymph tumbling along the bottom will. The ideal situation for weighted nymph fishing occurs when the water is slightly off-color. Not dirty, mind you, but about the shade of weak tea with just a spot of cream in it. Cloudy water prevents the trout from seeing your silhouette clearly. This advantage is extremely important when fishing the weighted nymph because to do it well requires short casts and a good sense of touch; it's best to be close to the fish.

Unlike other forms of sunken fly fishing, the weighted nymph is best fished upstream. This program calls for a short cast, no more than 12 or 14 feet, that's designed to allow the nymph to tumble along the bottom in a drag-free attitude. Since you will seldom be able to see the nymph or the fish, a strike must be felt. The strike can come as a gentle "pull" or a solid jerk. But never assume that either sort of strike suggests the size of the trout. Very large trout will frequently take a nymph quite tenderly whereas small trout may hit with a vengeance.

When casting a nymph upstream, it should tumble along on or near the bottom in an unfettered manner. To achieve this and be able to see or feel the strike, excess line must be stripped in with thumb and forefinger while the line coming from the first guide is held lightly under the forefinger or the rod hand. Simply allow the stripped line to fall near your wader tops in loose coils. If a fish takes, tighten the forefinger, pinching the line to the rod grip and crank the loose line onto the reel.

The trickiest part of drifting a nymph along the bottom is deciding how much weight to add to the leader. In shallow water of two feet or less, with a mild rate of flow, the weight of the nymph itself may be enough. Nymphs can also be tied with lead strips or wire totally hidden underneath the body material. At other times, in deeper or faster water, additional weight will be needed. Small split shot, wrap-around sinkers, or the currently popular "soft" lead can be used. Attach the weight no more than ten inches from the nymph for best drifting; any farther up the leader and too many hang-ups will occur, hang-ups that will feel like a strike. It may require some adding and removing weight until you find the perfect combination for a particular pool. The next pool might call for a different amount of lead due to the velocity and volume of water. The knowledgeable nympher will adjust sinker weight several times a day.

In spite of good technique, the angler using nymphs on the bottom will still get hung-up on rocks, sticks, and assorted debris. Some of these hang-ups will feel very much like strikes. The best plan is to strike at any touch or line stoppage. Yes, you'll sink the hook into a lot of strange things that aren't trout—but you'll be rewarded often enough to make it worthwhile.

Fishing Nymphs Close to the Surface

Nymphs that float on or near the surface can be highly effective when trout are "bulging," or making a sort of half-rise. Careful observation will reveal that the trout is not actually breaking the surface but only making the water bulge or hump-up as it seizes an insect. Ideally, the nymph should drift along in a suspended attitude. In quiet water greasing the first three feet of the leader with dry-fly floatant will do the trick. If the floating leader moves even an inch, strike. In faster water, a strike indicator in the form of a tiny piece of plastic foam or one of the

commercial pinch-on plastic discs works perfectly. Placement of the indicator controls the depth of the nymph.

When fishing nymphs on or near the surface, cast up and beyond the fish. Any movement on the part of the indicator is the signal to strike . . . not hard though . . . just a firm *pull*. Trout taking such drifting nymphs usually do so positively and have the hook well inside their mouths by the time the angler reacts.

Nymph Patterns

Unlike traditional dry flies and wet flies, nymphs have not yet reached the point of standardization from region to region or from catalog to catalog. "Whitlock's scud" or dragonfly nymph doesn't look much like "Arbona's scud" or dragonfly. The addition of the surnames is about the only form of standardization with nymphs. The name Whitlock refers to Dave Whitlock, Arbona to Fred Arbona, both well-known anglers and fly innovators. There are many other nymph "inventions" tagged with the names of their creators.

One suggestion is to spend some time looking at fly catalogs to discover which nymphs look like those in your favorite waters. Another is to buy a selection of nymphs recommended for your area by one of the mail-order houses, such as Orvis, Thomas and Thomas, Pennsylvania Outdoor Warehouse, or Umpqua Feather Merchants in Oregon. The third, and probably the best idea, is to visit your local fly fishing shop and ask the clerk for his suggestions. He'll want you as a repeat customer, so you'll usually receive good advice.

As with wet and dry flies you'll need a selection of somber colors that suggest the real thing. Because nymphs are fished right down there in the trout's bailiwick, in a dead drift manner, bright, flashy colors are seldom useful.

There is an important exception to this. A hook wound with bright green yarn is a wonderful fish catcher on any stream that sees an annual appearance of measuring worms. These brilliant green worms, the ones that dangle from the trees during the summer months on gossamer threads, are choice trout food. For some reason, trout enjoy them just as much fished deep as they do on the surface. In fact, they seem to hit them with more confidence when fished as nymphs. Even on western streams, where measuring worms are nonexistent, a green or bright chartreuse nymph will often do a land-office business.

At one time, dry flies were the favorite "show-off" types for fly tyers. Currently, it's the nymphs that are sparking the most highly creative fly offerings. Synthetic materials mixed with natural fur and feathers are being fashioned into near perfect duplicate. Anglers love 'em because they just look so great. And yes, they catch fish. Interestingly, they don't catch any more fish, and frequently not as many, as the nymphs that are tied somewhat on the scruffy side. Tip: Tie or buy some nymphs made with natural fur bodies. The real stuff reflects available light in a different way than do the synthetics. They simply look "buggier." Unlike some other flies, the more they're fished with—to a point—the better they seem to produce.

FISHING STREAMER FLIES

Since all trout are predators and feed on small fish of many kinds, it follows that a fly type suggesting a minnow would be a logical choice. It sure is. As an attention-getter for trout of heroic proportions, nothing works better than a streamer fly on most waters. The long, graceful feather and hair wings of streamer flies appeal to both angler and fish. Any trout fisherman's fly box should have a selection of streamer flies, and they should be used more often than they are; which raises an odd question.

It's paradoxical that many anglers carry streamers but seldom use them. If streamers are so effective on big trout (as most authorities concur), why aren't they used more? The problem may be that fishing them well is a "busy" method and requires some extra rod manipulation. That's true—but it's not *that* difficult.

A streamer fly is cast across and downstream much like a wet fly and then retrieved by stripping the line with the off-hand. The line is al-

lowed to slide beneath the index finger of the rod hand. By making short, quick strips, the fly can be made to dart nervously. By slowing the stripping action or increasing the length of each pull, the pulsating action of the fly can be altered. The angler is attempting to suggest a fleeing or injured minnow. By mixing retrieve styles, a streamer fly can be made to do all sorts of tricks.

A streamer can also be fished on or near the surface or at nearly any depth desired. As with wet flies and nymphs, lead foil or wire can be

Boulder in foreground is a classic trout lie. Author approaches carefully and is about to cast his streamer behind the rock. Streamers should be retrieved in short, choppy jerks to suggest a fleeing minnow.

wound around the hook shank before the fly is tied, or weight can be added to the leader. Allowing the fly to sink before beginning the retrieve is a good stunt to try in deep pools.

Character of the water and the mood of the fish will usually determine how to fish a streamer. A good way to begin is to retrieve quickly for a cast or two, then slow down until you're bringing the streamer back at a snail's pace, practically on the bottom. If you're not getting stuck on the bottom once in a while you're not doing it right.

Regardless of retrieve speed, *do not* get into the habit of applying the movement by jerking the rod tip. It's always best to move the fly by stripping the line and maintaining control of it underneath the index finger. Every time you jerk the rod tip, the line tends to sag between rod tip and the surface of the water. If a trout strikes while the line is sagging, you may see the strike but you won't feel it. Another good habit worth acquiring is to keep the rod tip no more than a foot from the surface of the water while stripping. This also helps to avoid a sagging line. Trout can smack a streamer quickly and be gone without feeling the hook point if there's too much slack line. Be ready to strike at all times.

As with any sort of fly, a strike to a streamer can occur the split second the fly enters the water. Not infrequently, a wary fish will follow a streamer a great distance before making a commitment. Many trout, and big ones too, will trail a streamer into extremely shallow water. It figures. When a trout is chasing real minnows, it has learned that herding them into shallow water allows a better chance at grabbing one than does a frantic race in the depths. The minnows' options of escape narrow greatly in water that's inches deep instead of feet. For this reason, fish each cast carefully and keep the fly moving until the last possible moment.

With dries and wet flies, a missed strike usually means that particular fish is lost for the day or at least for the next several hours. If it feels the hook point, forget it. If you see an underwater flash or a swirl behind a streamer fly, however, and you don't connect, you still have a second chance. Make another cast immediately to the original spot and repeat the action that caused

interest the first time. If the fish wasn't spooked, it's a good bet that it'll take another crack at your fake minnow.

In fast water, an extremely active technique is to cast the steamer up-current on a short line and bring it back very quickly. It's very difficult to do this with more than twenty-five feet of line. But when it can be managed, trout seem to become excited by the quick look at a fleeing minnow. They also "know" that if they're going to catch it, they must do so in a hurry. This technique is particularly effective on rainbow and cutthroat trout.

Many of the same retrieving nuances and styles that work with wet flies can also be applied with streamers. Unlike dry flies, which catch more fish when they're doing nothing except floating along, streamers must be given motion. As already noted, fishing them requires some effort and creativity, but they'll also coax the big ones.

Streamer flies are tied to suggest minnows. Some are somber and some are flashy. Standard flies for salmon in the Northeast, streamers will catch trout everywhere if fished properly.

The famous Muddler Minnow streamer. If there's one essential streamer pattern, this is it. Stock your fly box with several in sizes 6, 8, and 10.

Streamer Fly Patterns

Streamers fall into two general categories—the suggestive patterns and the attractors. The first category refers to those flies that resemble small fish (more or less) and the second to flies that are colorful attention-getters. The most famous of these is the Mickey Finn. Created by master angler John Alden Knight at least seventy-five years ago, the Mickey Finn consists of a silver tinsel body with bands of red and yellow deer hair as a wing. Usually tied on a long-shank hook, the Mickey Finn looks like no minnow that ever swam. It has, however, been the undoing of millions of trout. The other side of the streamer fly coin is best exemplified by the equally famous Muddler Minnow. Another angling legend, Don Gapen, first tied the Muddler to suggest the bottom-dwelling sculpin minnow and it worked splendidly. It still does. Basically a brown fly, the Muddler has a clipped deer-hair head, a turkey feather wing mixed with more brown hair, and a gold tinsel body. These two streamer patterns should be in your box on any trout water.

The other three "must" streamer patterns for trout fishing anyplace in the world would be the Grey Ghost, the Black Ghost, and the Blacknose Dace. I mention these because they're readily obtainable, but a wide assortment of special streamers have proven their worth as well. Dave Whitlock's Sculpin series are all excellent producers, as are the Keith Fulsher Thunder Creek streamers. John Gierach's Bucktail Muddlers, with their big eyes, are wonderful and so are the Matuka-style streamers that originated in New Zealand.

As with nymphs, there are hundreds of regional favorites that catch a heap of trout, so it's always wise to watch and listen to the local talent.

FLY FISHING SMALL STREAMS

For those unfamiliar with small-stream angling, the suggestion of a fly rod for such work may come as a surprise. In outdoor magazines, films, and video tapes, we see the graceful fly-rodder extend those long casts to drop a fly some seventy yards away and wonder how in the world such a technique would have any application on a brushy brook. The obvious question is, "wouldn't one's fly spend most of its time being stuck in the bushes?" Sure it would, if a lot of long-range casting were attempted, but this is a small stream and even the expert can't expect to make long casts. What must be done is to switch the fly quickly using a roll cast or the easy-to-master bow-and-arrow cast. Here's how:

Keeping a low profile by crawling or duck-walking into position, about a rod's length from the pool, pull enough line, including the leader, from the reel to reach the hotspot and hold the bend of the hook between thumb and forefinger. Flex the rod like a bow, and aim the fly by sighting down the taut line. Pop! Let the fly go and, like an arrow, it will be delivered to the right spot. Yes, it requires a little practice, but you can do this indoors during the off season or in your yard or nearby vacant lot. It's surprising how useful and effective this technique can be on tiny streams. The bow-and-arrow cast can also be used with natural baits such as crickets, grasshoppers, and small garden worms.

9

Fishing Lakes and Ponds

When discussing lakes and ponds some agreement must be reached on the difference between them. Most dictionaries are not very helpful. In typical dictionary style we're informed that a pond is "smaller than a lake" and a lake is usually "larger than a pond." Anglers should be a bit more definite, because the fish in small, shallow ponds behave much differently from those in large, deep lakes. For ease of discussion, let's classify all bodies of water covering less than fifty acres as ponds and those larger as lakes. The number fifty is also a useful unit of measurement in establishing what's "deep" and what isn't. Any lake or pond that has depths of fifty feet or more is *deep*. However, to avoid constant repetition, I've referred to all bodies of still water as "lakes" unless I'm making a distinction between the two.

The basic difference between finding fish in lakes and finding them in brooks, streams, or rivers is that in still water they can be anyplace. As noted in the previous chapter, fish in moving water can be located with considerable success once we learn something about "reading the water." The undercut banks, submerged logs, and other natural obstructions that alter the water's downhill flow are easily observed clues. Gazing across a flat sheet of still water doesn't tell us much. We must do our detective work in other ways.

The time of year is important in having some idea of where to fish a lake. Water temperature is more often than not the key to knowing where to try first and at what depth. This is true with all species (bass and walleyes are very temperature sensitive) and much more important in lakes than in moving water. All the trouts and chars can be found in lakes. In some parts of the world, still water is the best place to fish for them. They move from depth to depth as the seasons change; finding a comfortable temperature is second only to finding food. Fortunately for the angler, the trout's food supply in most lakes is often found where the trout are most comfortable.

ICE-OUT FISHING

In lakes that freeze from shore to shore, the three-week period immediately following "ice-out" can produce the best fishing of the year.

On many lakes, a good place to start trolling is along a shoreline rimmed with rocky bluffs. Weave the boat along the bluffs, following the contour of the bottom.

Cold water and a limited supply of food brings hungry trout close to the surface and into the shallow bays. It would be impossible to say exactly what would be the best lure, bait, or fly at this time, but garden worms, live minnows, or canned salmon eggs are excellent baits fished with spinning or fly tackle.

If you aren't fishing with a guide or someone who has fished the lake previously, you may have to search for a while, but it's not that difficult. An electronic fish finder is a helpful tool in locating fish and determining depth, but it is not essential. Chances are, in the early part of the season, the trout won't be too deep, and drifting with the breeze with your bait hanging at about the six-foot mark should produce a strike. For this kind of drift fishing a plastic bobber will hold your bait at the required depth and indicate a strike as

well. Beginning anglers, especially kids, love to use bobbers because it's fun to watch them dance. When the bobber goes under, set the hook!

If you or your companion is already familiar with the lake, you'll have some idea where to cast artificial lures. If you're not, drifting and casting here and there is one way to start and may lead to your discovering a hotspot. If it's a small pond, and you can easily see from one shore to the other, freelance drifting is as good as any method. If there's more surface area to cover, trolling may be called for.

To some anglers, trolling a lure behind a moving boat seems a simple-minded pursuit. (Well, I suppose all fishing seems simple-minded to those poor folks who've never tried it.) The truth is, trolling is an easy way to catch fish, but it requires some angling savvy and experimentation. During the spring, when warmer surface temperatures draw the trout up from the icy bottom, usually a steady trolling speed that keeps the lure moving at about six feet deep is effective. As spring becomes summer and then *hot* summer, you have to troll your lures deeper and deeper. A return to surface fishing will take place again in the late fall. There's a good rule of thumb for determining how deep to troll. If the water temperature a foot below the surface is above 58 degrees, troll deeper than 6 feet. If it's above 65 degrees, troll *much* deeper.

TROLLING AND JIGGING FOR LAKERS

Whereas most trout seem to prefer water between 52 and 60 degrees, lake trout choose colder water for their comfort zone. If you're fishing for lakers, which prefer water below 50 degrees, you'll have to troll deeper, or drop live baits or jigs to the bottom.

There are several ways to sink a lure below 20 feet. The easiest is simply to stop the boat and allow the weight of the lure to carry it down to the bottom or close to it and then go forward under motor or oar power. Eventually, the lure will glide back towards the surface and you'll have to stop and let it sink again. This is a busy way to fish but it works well at times. Lake trout on or near the bottom must think the lure is something good to eat and is about to escape; they usually grab it as it begins its ascent. Be alert however, as line is being payed off the reel during the drop. Not infrequently, a laker will strike just as the lure comes into its line of vision. If you drop the lure slowly, at a steady rate, a slight twitch in the line is the signal to strike.

This kind of stop-and-start trolling is best done with large spoons and wobblers or sinking minnow-shaped lures. Experienced lake trout guides have known for years that changes in trolling speeds, stopping between speed shifts, sometimes works wonders. If a steady trolling speed is maintained, the lure will soon be on or near the surface. The buoyancy of the line itself

This lake trout was found with the aid of an electronic fish-finder. Standard baitcasting tackle is ideal for trolling.

will make this happen. Even the smooth, seemingly waterproof monofilament line everyone uses today will float until it absorbs some water—sometimes as much as 15 percent of its weight. That's why lures ride deeper as the fishing day progresses.

If a pattern develops and you have a strike when the boat passes over a particular spot, it's a good idea to stop there and try a bit of deep jigging. As the words suggest, this is done with a jig, a lure with a lead head and a tail of deer hair, synthetic hair, plastic, pork rind, or strip of fish belly. The technique is not complicated. The jig is simply dropped to the bottom; you'll know when it gets there because the line will stop running from the reel. Reel the line up taut and jerk the rod tip upwards with a quick jab. Allow the jig to drop again, crank the reel handle about three or four times and bounce the lure again. The idea is to jerk-jerk-jerk the jig in a lifelike

Fishing deep with lead-headed jigs like these is a good technique during hot weather. Lake trout prefer cold water and tend to move into the depths in summer.

way, hoping that the lake trout will think it's dinner time.

Another method of getting lures down deep is through the use of solid wire or lead-core line. Solid wire is just that, and was once standard trolling gear on many lakes where lake trout are the major game fish. Wire line works, but it's a pain in the neck to handle. A slight kink when winding in on the reel or lowering a lure for jigging or trolling can ruin the day if another reel loaded with wire is not at hand. Lead-core line is much easier to use, and many weighted-line fanciers prefer it over wire. However, lead-core line, like mono, tends to ride-up as trolling speed increases. Slowing down from time to time will help keep the lure deeper.

Tying a piece of lead-core onto a fly line is an excellent way to troll a streamer fly or lure when pursuing lake trout, landlocked salmon, or other trout when they are not close to the surface. A ten-foot piece of lead-core line will sink a six-foot leader and streamer fly down to ten feet or more at moderate trolling speed. More lead-core can be added if you want to go deeper or less if you want to try casting the fly. Be aware, however,

that attempting to cast much more than twelve feet of lead-core line on the end of a standard fly line requires perfect technique. Even the experts can't manage a great cast every time, and getting smacked in the head with ten feet of lead-core line is uncomfortable, to say the least. The most widely available brand of lead-core line is Cortland's, appropriately named Ker-Plunk.

Using lead sinkers to get a lure down to lake trout lairs is easy and productive. If you find yourself switching lures frequently, sinkers can be quickly attached and removed. If you prefer not getting overly involved in knot tying, rubber-cored sinkers are a good choice. They're available in most tackle stores and can be placed at any spot on the line. They don't damage the line and are quickly removed. They come in an assortment of weights.

Sinkers with loops and swivels in various shapes and sizes are useful trolling aids. They must be tied onto the line at some point and then to the short section of line (or leader) to which your lure or bait is attached (see illustration). The major problem in using sinkers of this type is that once a fish is hooked and brought to the

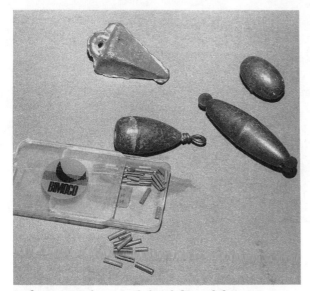

Sinkers are often vital for fishing lakes. Here are several useful types. Long, rubber-cored sinker at right is especially handy, as it may be attached and removed without damaging the line or tying knots.

FISHING WITH DOWNRIGGERS

The use of downriggers for trolling at depths below ten feet has become standard procedure on large lakes. It took a while to convince some of the traditionalists, but using downriggers for all species that spend some time in deep water is by far the best way to catch them. This is certainly true with all of the Pacific salmon that have been relocated to the Great Lakes and the lake-dwelling trout. The lake trout, togue, mackinaw, gray trout, or whatever local name it's known as, is a sucker for a steadily moving spoon, spinning lure, or plug.

The downrigger outfit basically consists of a winch containing a hundred feet or more of thin cable attached to a heavy weight. This winch is bolted or clamped to the side of the boat. A release clip on the weight holds the line that comes from the fishing reel. Ten or twelve feet of line, with lure attached, is payed out and the line is clipped to the weight. The weight is then lowered to the desired trolling depth and, as it's being dropped, additional line is payed from the reel. The fishing rod is then placed in a rod holder, and the reel is cranked until there's a deep bend in the rod. The reason for the deep bend is to cause the rod to snap up tight when a fish strikes, jerking the lure free from the clip. The fish frequently hooks itself. The angler then removes the rod from the holder and battles the fish without the heavy sinker on his line.

boat the length of the line between sinker and lure is critical. Since the tied-in sinker won't pass through the rod guides, the line next to the lure must be short enough to allow the fish to be grabbed or netted. This can be difficult. The compounding factor is that the length of line from sinker to lure must be long enough to allow the lure to wobble freely and not be so close to the lure that it spooks the fish. The best solution is to have a long-handled net on board, a five-footer at least.

Trolling rig with a three-way swivel allows the lure to wobble freely and prevents it from hanging up on the bottom. By changing sinker weight, you can fish at various depths.

This big laker went for a deep-running lure trailed behind a downrigger. Note whitish spots—the typical marks on a lake trout.

one reason: there is an abundance of fish food in the form of smaller fish. Smaller lakes and ponds are not always this food rich, and consequently the fish are smaller. In these waters, smaller lures, lighter tackle, and more refined techniques must be applied. But that's the wonderful thing about angling; it's never exactly the same. There is an infinite number of variables that makes the challenge ever changing.

TROLLING SMALL PONDS

Trolling a small pond with spinning or casting tackle and small lures or natural bait can be highly productive. You don't need much extra gear, just the basic tackle and a pair of oars or an electric motor. A good way to begin is to tie on a small line and make a forty-foot cast, then run the boat at a speed just fast enough to keep the line taut. It makes little sense to discuss trolling speed in terms of miles per hour because wind, size of boat, weight of lure, and so many other variables come into play. At first, it's more important just to keep the line taut and the lure in motion.

Trolling with live bait is done in the same manner except that boat speed should be reduced a bit so as not to lose the less durable minnow or worm.

Unless you see surface activity—some swirls or splashes—it's best to begin trolling close to the shoreline and gradually move towards the center of the pond. Minnows and other natural foods are usually found in shallow water. This is not an absolute truth in some lakes because of bars, rocky shoals, and other bottom structures that may cause abrupt changes in depth. It's possible to find an extremely shallow area smack in the middle of the lake or pond. That shallow spot could be precisely where the fish are in cool weather or during the early morning hours. During the heat of summer, a good rule of thumb is to try the deeper spots. As opposed to finding a shallow bar in the middle of an impoundment, it's not unusual to discover the deepest water in some ponds and lakes to be immediately adjacent to the shoreline. This is often the case in

There's a lot of teamwork necessary when downrigging. One or two downriggers can be handled by a lone angler, but it's much easier with two or more on board. Trying to operate the boat, set the lines, and pay out line from winch and fishing reel at the same time can be compared to one of the comedy routines in the old silent movies. There's a lot going on, and extra hands help spread the work around.

In ponds and lakes all of the other trout species can be caught using the same methods and techniques as those used for lake trout. This is very much the case in large, deep lakes where brown and rainbow trout can grow to heroic sizes of 15 or more pounds. Trout in that size range are caught in the Great Lakes and a few other large lakes with considerable frequency for

Downrigger reel allows you to fish deep without having to fight a heavy weight on the line. The line is attached to a weight with a release clip which snaps free when a fish grabs the lure.

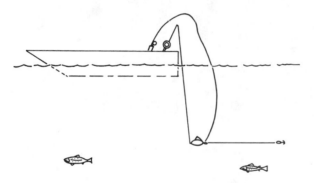

hilly or rocky terrain. If you are familiar with the pond you've got a leg up on the other guy; if not, a sonar depth-finder is a valuable tool.

When trolling a small pond, try different depths, change trolling speeds, and switch lures or bait frequently, just as you would on a large lake. Because one technique worked the last time, it doesn't mean it's the magic formula. Trout alter their feeding habits, food preferences, and comfort zones at the slightest change in temperature, wind direction, or water level. Barring extreme weather conditions, hot or cold, it's a safe bet that fish will want to eat at some time during a fishing day. Don't worry about being there at the "best" time. Most of us can't pick and choose all of our fishing days. We must go fishing when we can, and if we experiment fish can be taken almost any day.

LURES FOR TROLLING

Spinners

Lures for trolling small lakes and ponds include nearly everything that wears a hook, but some types have consistently proven to be much better than others.

One of the most famous spinners is the Mepps Aglia lure. The Mepps line of lures contains several blade shapes and a wide variety of sizes. In general, the thicker the blade the deeper the lure will drop. Other brand names found on effective spinning lures are C. P. Swing, Rooster Tail, and Felmlee. Lures of this sort are designed to allow the blade to rotate as the lure is trolled. This presents a flashing sparkle as the lure moves through the water. The trailing hook is usually a small treble (three-barbed) concealed beneath a skirt of squirrel-tail hair or synthetic material.

Blade color or finish and the color of the hook-covering material come in a nearly unlimited selection. To the first-time tackle store visitor, the choice of colors is mind bending. Can you fish *really* be that selective? Well, yes and no. That doesn't seem like much of an answer, but it's the best one I can come up with. On most days a

*Spinning lures that may be cast or trolled. Rotating blades of spinners and spoons
(next photo) can twist line, so it's advisable to attach them with a snap swivel.*

trout that's in the mood to strike something will probably do so regardless of the color. At other times the only lure that will catch them must be green and white (or you name it) with a silver blade. And then, anglers have preferences too. It doesn't matter what the fish think, some very good fishermen insist on using a particular color and do well with it. Is there some place to start if one doesn't have a tacklebox full of experience?

My favorite spinning lure consists of a silver blade with a natural squirrel-tail skirt tied on with red thread, or perhaps a spot of red on the blade. Next would be a gold-finished blade with a black skirt or a soft rubber minnow imitation. Plain old black and white is another regular item in my tacklebox. The most important thing to

remember is that big fish eat little fish. Since we're trying to suggest little fish with most lures, it follows that they should be dark on the top side and light on the bottom—the reason being that 99.9 percent of all baitfish are similarly shaded. The logic for a spot of red is that it suggests blood. The smallest trout is fully as aggressive as the largest shark in the ocean when it comes to taking advantage of wounded prey. A crippled baitfish is easier to catch and eat than a swift, healthy one.

Spoons

Wobbling spoons have long been good trout catchers in ponds and lakes. The most famous of these is the Dardevle family of lures. They are made in sizes ranging from about 1½ inches long to some monsters that are about the size of a small canoe paddle. Large ones, those over 3½ inches long, are best saved for large lakes and huge fish. Those measuring from 2 to 3 inches are the right size for small lakes and ponds. That's not a fast rule, however. If you discover that the average size of the common baitfish in the water you're fishing is larger or smaller, adjust the lure size accordingly.

There are dozens of companies making spoon-type lures; all of them have caught trout at one time or another. Check the photos and you'll notice that spoons come in a wide variety of shapes and colors. Competition is keen in the lure business, and there aren't many duds among those offered. The poorly made ones just don't survive. The things to watch for when buying lures are good-quality hooks, smoothly finished eyes (where the line or swivel attaches), and a well-done paint job or metallic finish.

Good choices to lead off with are red and white, solid silver, yellow and red, and some sort

The famous Daredevle lure has probably seduced more lake trout than any other. Be sure to have at least one in your tacklebox when you go fishing.

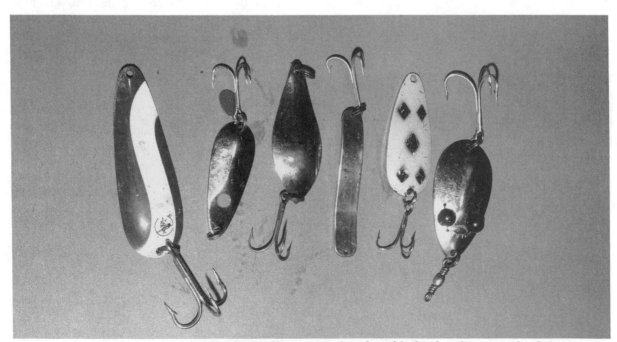

An assortment of spoons. Usually equipped with treble hooks, these standard lake lures catch more fish when the points are kept sharp.

of metallic blue or green. After that, what's your favorite color?

Plugs

The minnow-shaped lures, or plugs, as they're commonly called, are the third most important group for lake fishing. In some waters they are considered the most important. Plugs by Rapala, Rebel, Cordell, Heddon, Arbogast, and a dozen other well-known names have caught tons of trout. They do because they look like little fish, and the trout must think so too. Practically all of these lures wobble from side to side as they're being trolled or retrieved, and what separates one from the other is the degree of wobble. No, that's certainly not a scientific measurement, but it's highly important to the manufacturers and can be to the fish. On most of these lures there's a little plastic or metal lip beneath the head end that causes them to wiggle as they move forward. The shape and size of this lip determine that degree of wobble.

Some of these lures are designed to ride close to the surface; others are weighted to coast along at greater depths. As with other types of lures, only on-the-spot practice will determine which is best on a given day. As with spinning lures and spoons, larger plugs are generally more productive in big lakes and smaller ones in ponds. Many of these lures are available in "pocket" sizes, and a good rule is to begin small, with, say, a 3-incher. It's worth noting here that small trout of 12 inches or less are not adverse to striking a lure half their length, nor will 2-footers turn down a tiny lure of 2½ inches or even smaller.

Minnow-type lures should be selected to match the colors of the baitfish present in the lake. I like those with grayish or black backs and white or silver bellies. Those with some gold on their sides are also effective. I'm quite fond of lures with perchlike stripes if the back is dark and the belly is creamish or white. Nicely painted lures that are designed to suggest small trout can be absolutely deadly in some lakes and ponds. Like most predatory fish, large trout are not at all squeamish about eating their offspring.

While plugs are made in every imaginable shape, size, and color, the basic type we'll consider here are those that dive when trolled or retrieved. These are either wide-lipped lures or those shaped, more or less, like a banana. Lures of this configuration will dive deep when pulled through the water and are excellent fish catchers

Three Rapala lures of the swimming-minnow type. These lures are very effective for trout and salmon.

when trout are hanging in the mid-depths. These lures will dive to ten or twelve feet when trolled (depending on boat speed) and deeper if a sinker is attached a few feet above the lure.

If the fish are not on or near the bottom (where deep jigs or downriggers are the solution) or close to the surface where they can be reached with spinning lures or swimming plugs, diving lures are the logical choice. Diving Rapalas, Rebels, Lazy Ikes, Flatfish, and several of the crayfish style are possible choices. Select colors and sizes as you would for other lures, but be sure to include some in a dull brown or olive color, because trout eat crayfish too. If the diving lure comes close to the bottom (and it will in water less than ten feet deep) you could enjoy the best fishing of the year!

Tip: When trolling lures of all types, don't assume that because you felt a solid tug that the fish is automatically hooked. Strike back with a sharp jab and crank the reel handle at the same time until you feel resistance. A fish striking a trolled lure will sometimes move towards the boat and the line will go slack. You must get the loose line on the reel quickly in order to tighten up.

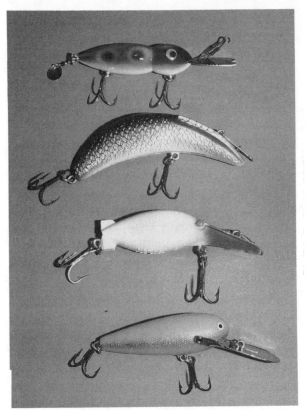

Lures with long front lips tend to dive deep when trolled. They can be trolled off the rod or, for maximum depth, with a downrigger.

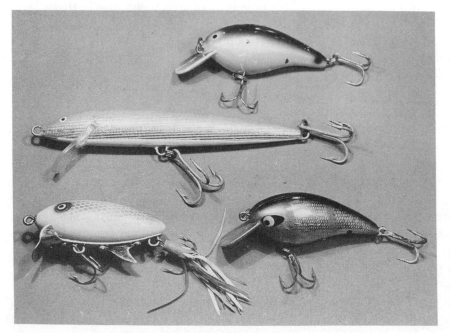

For a change of pace, try lures with a fat profile. They sometimes produce when the slim fellows don't work. Switch lures until you find one that pleases the fish.

This big lake trout grabbed a swimming lure that was almost 6 inches long, probably mistaking it for a large baitfish.

TROLLING WITH A FLY ROD

In early spring and late fall, when cool temperatures bring the fish near the surface, trolling with a fly rod can be highly productive. It's the traditional method for catching landlocked salmon in New England lakes and ponds, and it works for other species too. Trout of all sizes will go for a trolled streamer fly or smaller wet flies.

If you see fish rising to take surface insects, dry flies are called for. For the moment, however, let's stick with trolling. There are days when a fly dragged behind a boat some forty feet will be all that's needed to catch trout or salmon. But fish being the fickle creatures they are sometimes demand some variations. One of the best of these is achieved by bouncing the rod tip as the fly swims along. Lifting and lowering the rod will

cause the fly to pulsate and appear more lifelike. Remember, what you're trying to do is create the appearance of a live minnow. The jiggling and dancing that you impart to the fly can be subtle or violent, and both approaches are needed at times. When you find a combination of movements that do the job, mentally catalog it and use that technique on similar days.

If the fish are close to the surface, you can use a standard floating line. If they're a bit deeper, a sink-tip line or a full sinking line is a better choice. Tying in a section of lead-core line, as previously discussed, is another way to sink the fly, as is adding some rubber-core or split-shot sinkers.

In small ponds one of my favorite trolling routines is to rig a trio of small wet flies and move the boat or canoe with paddle or oars. I know that muscle power is somewhat out of style today, with such a wide variety of electric and gasoline motors available, but there's a great advantage in not using these at times. The human touch at the oars or paddle delivers a peculiar action to trolled flies. They drop a bit deeper as the paddle is lifted and rise a few inches when the power stroke is applied. The movement is not unlike that of an aquatic insect struggling to reach the surface. If such a natural occurrence is taking place, it's a fair bet that the trout are watching. The neat part of this technique is that if you move ahead just fast enough to keep a big sag out of the trolling line and leader, a trout that grabs the flies will usually hook itself. As a precaution against a powerful strike jerking your rod overboard, it's a good idea to tie a stout cord around the rod handle with the other end tied to a boat cleat or seat. Having lost a rod and reel, I learned the hard way.

In the chapter on fly fishing, there is a drawing showing how to rig three flies on droppers for this kind of trolling. But some suggestions on fly choices for lake fishing are appropriate here. If you actually see some aquatic insects where you're fishing, it makes sense to select patterns that resemble the naturals. But such matching the hatch isn't always necessary on ponds and lakes. Unlike trout in moving water, the fish in still water take a fly more casually because it's not

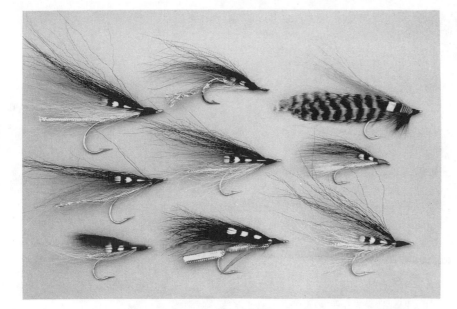

Trout and salmon will strike trolled flies that resemble minnows. At times they'll prefer them to larger metal or wooden lures. It pays to experiment.

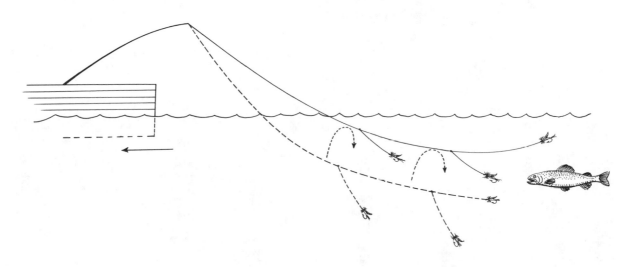

Trolling wet flies behind an oar-powered boat can be highly effective. The undulating flies often are irresistible to trout that are near the surface.

going to be carried away by the current. They don't seem to be so fussy and, in fact, are often more attracted to flashier patterns and colors.

Excellent choices are those with some gold or silver ribbing on the bodies and a touch of orange or red somewhere in their make-up. I am especially fond of the ancient Professor and Grizzly King patterns and, where there are brook trout, the well-known Royal Coachman. Almost any patterns with peacock herl bodies are good lake flies, with the Governor and Hardy's Favorite at the top of the list. I realize these patterns may sound old-fashioned to today's scientific anglers, but they work.

10

Pacific Salmon

As the name suggests, the inclusive heading "Pacific salmon" refers to those fish of the salmon clan that inhabit the Pacific Ocean and those rivers that flow to it. But since the mid-60s a thriving fishery for coho and chinook salmon has developed in the Great Lakes. An abundance of alewifes and smelt, two excellent forage species, provide a food source that grows big salmon in these lakes.

Regardless of where you find them, in fresh or salt water, the two most important salmon species, the coho and the chinook, will respond to similar angling techniques. In the near-shore waters of the Pacific and in the off-shore depths of the Great Lakes, salmon are active feeders and seldom turn down an opportunity to charge into a mass of baitfish. Moving about in small schools, the salmon feed at the same time, and there's fast action for the angler who's at the right place at the right time.

The chinook salmon is the most important of the West Coast species and is at least in a tie in the Great Lakes with the coho for popularity awards. It is the largest of the salmons (east or west) and has been known to weigh over 100 pounds. The current average is somewhere between 12 and 18, but enough whoppers of 30 or more are taken each year to make this fish a real heavyweight contender. The same trolling and casting techniques that work with cohos are appropriate for chinooks, but they'll frequently be found at greater depths.

The same baits and lures suggested for cohos may be used, but chinooks often take much larger offerings. Baitfish up to 10 inches are not too big for chinooks, and spoons and lures can be nearly as long. Chinooks are also vulnerable to being attracted to flashing strips of metal known as "dodgers." A string of three or more spinning blades a foot or more in front of the lure or bait will attract chinooks in deep, dark water. Chinooks are extremely moody fish and sometimes require a lot of lure changing and adjusting for depth.

While the coho and chinook are the preferred targets of most salmon anglers, the sockeye and pink salmons deserve more attention than they receive. Because we see them mostly in cans on

A beautiful, bright chinook, or king, salmon from British Columbia waters. Note the missing scales where the fish was rubbed by the line as it was being boated. The scales on a fish in saltwater are very loose but firm up when it enters freshwater.

supermarket shelves, some anglers don't consider them to be worthwhile sport fish. From Washington to Alaska, the Pacific coastal streams and rivers play host to millions of these salmon each year—and they're willing strikers.

The sockeye salmon is probably the major link of the food chain in scores of West Coast rivers. The rainbow trout and other fish eat their eggs. Gulls, terns, kingfishers, and ospreys eat the juvenile fish. Bears, including the big grizzly, feed on spawning adults; eagles, foxes, and other stream-side creatures clean up what's left of their meals. But still the sockeye survives in prodigious numbers.

You can't miss seeing sockeyes when they're in the river. The bright red flanks of the spawning males shine like neon lights. They are not active feeders during the spawning run but they'll take a pass at nearly any lure, fly, or drifting object that comes near them. A sockeye is the best

"beginner fish" in the world because of this. They are not flashy battlers like the coho or chinook, but they fight with great strength and tenacity. As a training exercise in fighting larger fish, landing a sockeye has no equal. If you lose one, there's another one ready to go.

Small spinning lures with a dash of red, pink, or orange are fatal attractions for sockeyes and so are streamer flies of the same colors. As a rule, sockeyes will hit a smaller lure than will cohos or chinooks.

The pink salmon's western range is about the same as the sockeye's, but they may not enter the same rivers. Where they do, the same lures and flies will coax them, and they're almost as strong as the sockeye. They don't run quite as large, with a big pink being about 4 pounds compared with an average sockeye at 5 or 6 pounds. Pink salmon have been stocked in the Great Lakes with some success, so it's possible to catch one

This Lake Erie coho salmon went for a trolled spoon moving just off the bottom.

Pink salmon are fond of small lures and flies. Like all salmon in freshwater, they seem to prefer lures in red and orange.

some place other than Pacific drainage waters. The heavily spotted tail—with larger spots than those on a rainbow trout—is the tip-off.

The food value of most Pacific salmon is excellent until they begin to deteriorate just before spawning. After they spawn, the flavor is very strong and not worth the cleaning effort. Personal tastes vary, of course, but I prefer Pacific salmon that are caught close to the ocean, well before spawning. They are oily fish, so broiling, poaching, and smoking are far superior cooking methods than baking or (perish the thought) frying.

LOCATING FISH

Finding salmon in the ocean can be extremely easy on certain days and as difficult as locating that proverbial haystack needle on others. Elec-

On any lake or ocean estuary, a flock of birds usually means there are baitfish below—and below them, hungry gamefish.

tronic fish finders can help, but the old saltwater angler's advice to look for the birds is as sure as anything. When a school of hungry salmon locates a school of herring, candlefish, or sardines near the surface, the terns and gulls are sure to see them. When *you* see the white birds diving and wheeling about, head for that spot. Casting, drifting, or trolling near bird activity is the best strategy.

If you own a boat or have a fishing pal who does, chasing birds is exciting and usually productive. It does require good boat handling, so if you're not sure of your seamanship, buying a spot on a charter boat is a better way to start.

When salmon are near the surface and into a feeding frenzy, drifting fresh or frozen baitfish, either whole or in chunks, near the school will usually work well. So will casting or trolling flashy metallic spoons, spinning lures with rotating blades, and many lures that resemble small

fish. To drift baits effectively requires that the boat be positioned so the prevailing tide pulls the baits through the feeding area. When trolling with lures or whole fish, moving along the edge of the active area is usually better than trolling through the obvious hotspot. Too much boat and motor noise may spook them, so stay on the edge of the school or try to plot a course that allows the lures to move across the leading edge of the feeding fish. If you decide to cast into the school, try to position the boat slightly in front and to one side of the surface activity.

When trolling for salmon, a most critical consideration is speed. Finicky salmon will strike a lure that's barely moving on some days and almost racing through the water on others. The boat operator is in control here and, if he's experienced, will try several trolling speeds searching for the right one. When a strike occurs, note the speed and return to that rate of travel.

A fresh or frozen sardine (or anchovy) is a deadly bait when rigged with a plastic bait holder. Note that the leader extends from the head of the bait holder and is embedded in the sardine's back.

CHOOSING THE RIGHT BAIT OR LURE

Baitfish in any given school usually average about the same size, but the average varies. Some schools will be made up of 4-inch fish while others may contain 6- to 8-inchers. The salmon may not show a preference but sometimes they do. If your bait isn't coaxing a strike, cut one in half or attach it to one of the popular bait holders that are sold in tackle stores. These are plastic sleeves that encase the head of a baitfish and are equipped with a hook or hooks that are then stuck into the body of the bait.

As they do on the West Coast of North America, the Pacific salmon species introduced to the Great Lakes seek running water when spawning time approaches. They enter many rivers that feed the Great Lakes and provide anglers with still more fishing opportunities. It is when these salmon enter the rivers that conservation agency

This chinook salmon struck the sardine bait still hanging from the leader. When the near shore waters are as calm as this, deep trolling is usually called for.

Large Rapalas and Rebels are favorite trolling and casting lures for chinooks and cohos. Red/silver and green/silver are usually effective colors, but try others if they don't bring a strike.

personnel gather enough eggs and milt to raise another batch of fingerlings for stocking. Some salmon may actually go through a natural spawning process but not enough of these offspring survive to provide worthwhile sport.

The transplanted salmon and the native Pacific salmon can be successfully fished for using similar techniques. Casting a spinning lure or plug across and downstream, then retrieving it against the current, is a standard method. A basic difference between fishing lures for salmon as opposed to trout is that salmon entering a river from a large lake or salt water stay close to the bottom, and you have to keep the lure down deep, occasionally touching the bottom as you reel it in. Coho salmon occasionally may rise to strike a lure near the surface, but chinooks seldom do.

Lures in any of the metallic colors (silver, gold, nickel, brass, copper) are good choices for salmon in rivers. A red or orange stripe is an added attractor. Spoons such as the Dardevle,

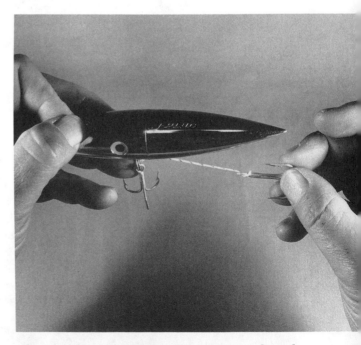

The famous J-Plug from Luhr Jensen is a lure designed to wobble and dart about like a frantic baitfish. A fine lure for chinooks and cohos in the salt.

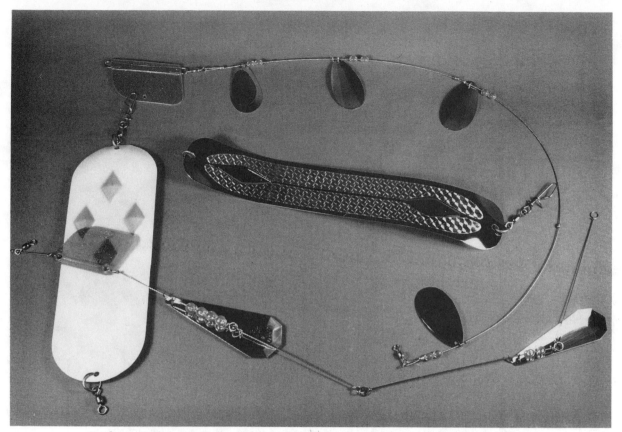

Dodgers and cow bells are flashing blades that are trolled in front of baits, lures, or flies. When fish are a bit sullen, these attention-getters often wake them up.

Johnson Silver Minnow, or Krockadile are good choices, as are revolving-blade spinning lures. While salmon are not always interested in small baitfish when they are on their spawning run, they will seize minnow-shaped lures. In fact, anglers on New York and Michigan rivers have reported some outstanding successes with Rebels, Rapalas, and a variety of lures painted to resemble small trout.

FLY FISHING FOR PACIFIC SALMON

Casting a fly into a school of salmon in the salt chuck may seem a futile occupation to those who have not tried it. It does call for some long-distance casting at times, and of course there's always some wind. In spite of the handicaps, a long, slinky fly that resembles a baitfish will often find a customer. Cast as close to the last swirl as you can manage and strip the line in smooth, long pulls. You won't have to be told if you get a strike. Hang onto the rod and let the fish run line off the reel. Hooking a big salmon in the salt is major league excitement. With an entire ocean to fight in, you'll quickly discover the value of a fly reel with a large capacity. The reel should hold a 9- or 10-weight fly line and 150 or more yards of backing. A tapered leader testing 8 or 10 pounds, about the same length as the rod, is a good choice.

In most pools, Pacific salmon will "hold," or rest, in the deeper parts until they reach their chosen spawning location. A sinking fly line and/

Pacific salmon go for flies too, and the best of these contain a lot of white and silver. Hooking a big salmon on a fly in saltwater often requires long-distance casting—and enough backing on your reel to outlast its powerful runs.

or weighted flies usually are required. Unless you've had experience with a weighted fly line, you'll find that it performs differently than a floating line. It is impossible to lift it from the water in one motion like a floating line. A sinking line must be retrieved and shot through the guides for each cast. Excessive false casting must also be avoided since it is tiring.

Saltwater flies for salmon should be tied on stainless steel or corrosion-proof hooks plated with nickel or cadmium. Sizes 1, 1/0, and 2/0 will cover most situations. The flies need not be complicated. As with lures, some silver tinsel on the body or built into the wing is suggested most of the time. Red and orange hairwings with a strip of blue or green on the top side are other good combinations.

Flies for river Pacific salmon don't have to be tied on nickel- or cadmium-plated hooks. They won't corrode. But many anglers prefer hooks plated with silver, nickel, or gold for the extra sparkle. There's some wisdom in this thinking, since getting the salmon's attention is often the major problem.

SALMON IN THE GREAT LAKES

Almost every technique used in saltwater also applies to the Great Lakes in one degree or another. But there are some major differences. Seasonal changes in these freshwater "oceans" cause greater variations in water temperatures. The salmon may be feeding on or near the surface or they may be at any depth. The number one task on any day is to determine the salmons' cruising level. Sonar fish-finders are a great help and can save countless hours cruising a lake. All professional charter boats on the Great Lakes are equipped with them; the more sophisticated of these devices are amazingly reliable. A skilled operator can not only distinguish individual fish on the screen or paper chart but determine species with considerable accuracy. With no tide line to indicate current, as there is in the ocean, freshwater salmon can be at any depth or in any part of the lake. When you find one, you'll usually find more.

In Chapter 9, on fishing lakes and ponds, the use of downriggers was discussed. Downrigging has become the standard method for salmon fishing in the Great Lakes. Fishing for salmon in big lakes is no different from fishing for large trout. Since both eat the same kinds of baitfish the same lures and techniques will do the job. In all of the Great Lakes it's possible to catch coho salmon, chinook salmon, brown trout, rainbow trout, and lake trout on the same day with the same lures. Because all of these fish are of the same general shape, it's important that the angler be able to identify them. Creel limits and minimum size requirements vary with the species in most states. Conservation officers do not usually accept faulty identification as an excuse. Be aware. The identification drawings in this book will help, but a careful examination of the fish you catch is the best way of learning.

11

Atlantic Salmon

A review of that portion of Chapter 1 which deals with Atlantic salmon is suggested here because this fish is quite different from Pacific salmon. There is but one Atlantic salmon and, by law in North America, it may be fished for with flies only. This is the only fish that comes under such stringent angling regulations. This is not the case in other countries that offer Atlantic salmon fishing. (I find this a curious fact in Great Britain. The Brits make much of sporting ethics, but they permit fishing for Atlantic salmon with lures and bait.)

The Atlantic differs from the Pacific salmon in that it does not die after spawning. Some do, as a result of the rigors of the struggle needed to reach spawning waters, but the fish that manage to negotiate the return trip to the sea are revitalized quickly and may spawn again.

Atlantic salmon are pursued relentlessly on the high seas by commercial netters but never to my knowledge have more than a handful been caught in saltwater on hook and line. Atlantics don't react to sport fishing techniques even in the mouths of most rivers they enter, so fishing for them is totally a freshwater sport. And it is a grand one if you're lucky enough to be on a river when the fish are there and in a taking mood. No other fish caught in freshwater, except the steelhead trout, runs so fast or jumps so high when hooked.

There is much tradition, history, and mystery involved in Atlantic salmon angling. Some old hands at the sport would have you believe that catching one is akin to being knighted. On some rivers, at certain times, it can be difficult, but the basic fly-rodding method is quite simple. The confounding part is why they strike flies in the first place, and why they strike a particular fly when they do.

Not all authorities agree on the question of salmon feeding in freshwater. They don't chase and eat smaller fish while on their spawning trip. In fact, they don't appear to eat at all. The stomachs of salmon, prior to spawning, contain nothing. They will, however, rise to take insects from the surface but apparently don't swallow them. The best guess is that they rise to an artificial fly as a result of "remembering" their earlier days as

A 20-pound Atlantic salmon from the Eagle River in Labrador—a better-than-average fish by today's standards. Fishing for Atlantics is legal by fly only in all of North America.

When your first Atlantic salmon is tailed for you, you'll understand the allure of this unpredictable species. Although salmon do not eat on their spawning run, they will hit a fly.

juveniles when they did feed on river insects.

I make no apologies about my admiration for the Atlantic salmon. If I had to cast for one species the rest of my life (a situation not wished for) it would certainly be *Salmo salar*. The mysteries of Atlantic salmon are many, but why they take a fly is the most fascinating. It is the focal point of angling for the species. The same might be said for trout and many other fishes, but there's always the problem of desire that confuses the issue. Salmon may become hungry, but they don't actually eat when in freshwater prior to spawning. Trout will discontinue eating only

for a short time during their mating interlude. But during this time trout will seize flies, lures, and baits that drift over their spawning areas. They'll also grab sticks and leaves and all sorts of flotsam.

Since fish have no hands or fingers, they examine food by taking it in their mouths. It's not unlike a dog sniffing a bone, a tuft of grass, or a stranger's hand. If a fish has never seen a yellow and red streamer fly or a fake salmon egg, it must take the object in its mouth in order to determine its taste and texture. If it's not something it wishes to swallow, it ejects it in a flash. If the fish is not certain, it holds the strange thing a bit longer.

There are four reasons why fish take anything into their mouths: hunger, curiosity, anger, or whimsy. The first three are easily understood but the last may sound a bit far-fetched to a beginning angler. While all fish occasionally lunge at something just for the fun of it, Atlantic salmon seem to delight in such antics. I've seen dozens of Atlantic salmon rise to examine fly after fly before finally grabbing one. Some of these rises are behind, in front of, or over the top of the fly.

At other times, in similar locations, the salmon will take on the first rise. The false rises were not misses. If a salmon decides to take that fly, very few anglers are quick enough to take it away.

If any conclusion is possible, I'd say that Atlantic salmon don't act, they react. They simply respond to the pattern, size, and motion of the fly, and to other stimuli of the moment. With experience, an angler can try to duplicate fly pattern, size, or presentation with some degree of intelligence. Such application of reasoning pays off enough to let us know that we are on the

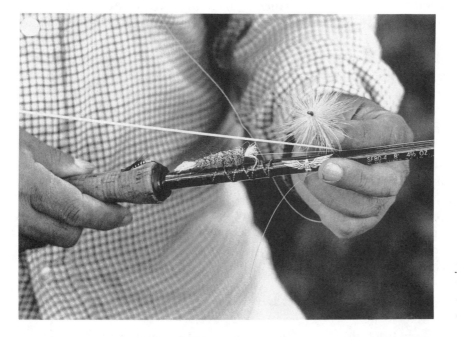

Three basic types of salmon flies (from left): a standard wet fly, a bug, and a fluffy dry fly. All will elicit strikes at the right times.

Wet flies cast for Atlantic salmon are handsome and heavily steeped in tradition. There is more than just fishing for this species to capture the imagination.

right track some of the time. But usually the Atlantic salmon angler cannot predict which fly will catch a fish on a given day. As one veteran put it, "There are no salmon fishing experts. No one lives that long, and the salmon aren't talking. But that's what makes it so much fun!"

THE FIRST CAST

The first cast for Atlantic salmon ought to be across and downstream. The cast should be made ten feet or so on the upstream side of the spot a salmon is expected to be. This is referred to as a "lie." These lies will remain constant from year to year in all rivers and are utilized by fish as regularly as the sun rises.

Identifying a lie is half the battle, but in most cases the first-timer will have the services of a guide to point them out. If you're on your own the first and often best choice will be very close to the edge of a pool where the water is smooth, just before it spills into rapids or small falls. Another choice location is immediately in front of or behind a large boulder or rock pile. Salmon seldom choose calm water as a resting place nor do they prefer heavy rapids. They will frequently be seen leaping and splashing at the base of a falls or a violent piece of water, but such fish generally are not catchable. They are vulnerable when they pause to rest. Only the salmon knows what it's looking for as a comfortable place to stop. The rate of flow must be to its liking.

As the first cast drifts over the hotspot, don't jiggle or move the fly at all. Simply allow the fly to coast naturally over the lie and watch. If a fish is there and it's in a taking mood, it will rise up in a sweeping curl, engulf the fly and turn towards its resting place. As it makes its turn, the force of the current pulling at the slack line will drive the hook point into the coorner of the salmon's jaw and a hook-up will be automatic. As the salmon feels the point it will probably race off in a wild rush that will sink the hook positively. Now, that was easy, wasn't it?

When fishing the traditional salmon wet fly with the dead-drift method, the routine just offered is the way most Atlantic salmon are hooked. But there are several variables that compound the situation. The novice Atlantic-salmon angler who's had experience with smaller trout and other species usually strikes too soon. As the fish rises in that peculiar "curling" manner, part of its body, dorsal fin, or tail—or all three—are likely to be visible. This sight and the accompanying splash often trigger the angler to jerk back his arm, expecting to feel the pull of a hooked fish. He won't. Steely nerves are needed to avoid this reaction. *Absolutely nothing should be done until a solid resistance is felt.* Then, raise the rod tip quickly, not violently, and you'll have hooked the fish.

Much of the time, over many lies, it will be necessary to strip the fly with the off-hand, allowing surplus line to gather around your waders. If such line and fly manipulation is required to coax a fish, make sure you keep the line beneath the forefinger of the rod hand. You can tighten up quickly if resistance is felt. If a dead drift or a slow stripping of the fly didn't work over a good-looking lie, strip a bit faster or allow the fly to sink a foot or so before beginning to strip. It can't be stressed enough that salmon are highly individual fish, probably more so than any other species, and what will make one fish respond won't get a tumble from the next one. It's a game of counter-moves.

SALMON ON DRY FLIES

While the Atlantic salmon shows a marked preference for a wet fly drifting just beneath the surface, it will come to a high-floating dry fly with gusto. Its desire to do this is a total mystery. Many salmon have been hooked on dry flies after refusing a hundred casts with wet flies. (To add to the puzzle, the reverse is also well documented.) Fishing a dry fly is basically the same for salmon or large brown trout. A drag-free float is essential. Drop the fly well above the suspected lie (or the fish, if you can see it) and allow it to float well beyond the spot before picking up for the next cast. Many times, salmon will turn to follow a dry fly for several feet before deciding to grab it.

If the salmon does take it, hooking can be

Wulff-type dry flies are popular and effective for Atlantics. They'll sometimes hit a dry after refusing a wet fly—and vice versa.

more of a problem than it is with wet flies. First off, there's probably slack line on the water, making a quick response difficult. But you've got to try. If you've kept your eye on the fly, strike the instant the fly vanishes. You may not see the fish's mouth open and the fly enter but strike anyway. If you're not looking at the fly, strike at the splash.

An effective trick involves a knot called the Portland, or riffling, hitch. A couple of half-hitches are tied in the leader and pulled tight *behind* the head of the fly. This causes it to skim across the surface. The resulting wake or "V" on the water will often bring a strike when nothing else will. As the half-hitches are tightened, care must be taken to make sure the leader stands at a right angle to the fly. By doing this, the fly acts like a miniature surfboard and glides on top of the water. This stunt works particularly well on fish that have risen but refused to take a totally sunken wet fly or a drifting dry fly.

Atlantic salmon don't seem to follow any set pattern. In addition to the ordinary wet flies and dry flies, plenty of salmon have been caught on flies of bizarre shapes, colors, and sizes. But, as noted, they are not actually feeding but only reacting.

A FLY SELECTION FOR ATLANTICS

In spite of the inconsistencies encountered in fishing for these magnificent fish, there are some fly patterns that have proven their worth over the years. Dark flies composed of a lot of black, brown, and gray materials are the favorites across much of eastern Canada. A touch of blue, red, yellow, or orange is sometimes valuable, as is a dash of silver or gold tinsel.

Favorite wet-fly patterns include: Blue Charm, Black Bear-green butt, Silver Grey, Cosseboom, Rusty Rat, Silver Rat, and Thunder and Lightning. With the exception of the first and last patterns, these are hairwing flies. All of these are available in stores and catalogs that supply salmon fishing equipment.

Effective dry flies include the Bomber, all of the Wulff patterns, Rat-faced McDougal, Trude, Adams, Buck Bug, and Badger Bivisible.

Size 6 is probably the most commonly used fly size on most Canadian rivers but that's not a hard rule. Size of the river, average size of the fish, and water conditions all determine size selection. But, as with all things dealing with Atlantic salmon, nothing is sure. Some large rivers that play host to a seasonal supply of big salmon are best fished with flies as small as 10s or 12s. On the other hand, smallish salmon of no more than 4 pounds will often rise for something as large as 3/0. Make every attempt to find out beforehand which sizes and patterns are recommended for the river you intend to fish.

It's wise for any tyro Atlantic salmon angler to listen to the locals, particularly to your guide. Certain flies are regionally popular for one good reason—they catch fish. As with bass plugs or offshore trolling lures, salmon flies come and go from year to year, with a few patterns lasting forever. It is a fact that particular color combinations appear to be much more effective on individual rivers than on others. The same is true of sizes. Most of the time the best advice is to tie on the pattern and size that your guide or experienced fishing companion suggests. But keep other options open.

Once on a Gaspé river that was running bank-full, the only salmon taken during a four-day stretch was hooked on a huge 4/0 Cosseboom. A young woman on her first Atlantic salmon adventure was stuck with a fly box full of size 6 flies that her friendly tackle store clerk had insisted she buy. Wanting to do things on her own, she refused the loan of a few larger flies, and much to the annoyance of her crusty guide, insisted on casting the smaller flies. You guessed it. The lass ended up being "high-rod" for the entire week with 5 fine salmon to her credit, one of them a 38-pounder, with all fish taken on size 6 flies.

A reverse of the story above took place on the famous Margaree River in Nova Scotia when low water caused the locals to switch to very small flies. A few fish were being taken but not enough to get excited about. Angling legend Vince Marinaro happened to be on the river at the time. On a whim, since he wasn't catching fish on anything, he decided to try a colorful fly named Tomah Joe. It was tied on a 3/0 hook and looked even larger in the water. Right again. Vince

Author's fly boxes contain a wide selection of patterns for Atlantics acquired over many years. Newcomers to the sport can catch salmon with fewer flies.

caught at least a half dozen salmon in three days by dragging that big fly in front of what had previously been dormant fish. Moral: Since salmon are essentially *reactive*, try to trigger a reaction by showing them something bizarre.

AFTER THE FISH IS HOOKED

Assuming that good things happen and you've hooked an Atlantic salmon, the same rules mentioned previously about handling trout apply—only more so. Upon feeling the hook, the majority of salmon make a wild race, peeling line off the reel at an alarming rate. If there is slack line to contend with, it's important to allow it to slip between the fingers freely until the fish is on the reel. Make no attempt to stop or check the run unless the salmon is headed for falls or rapids. You might be successful in applying the brakes but probably not. A better plan in this event is to allow the line to go slack and hope the pull of the current below the fish will cause it to turn.

If the fish jumps, and it probably will, drop the tip of the rod in order to create some slack line. This is known as "bowing" to the fish. In midair the full weight of the fish is applied to the leader. It may break. If the fish falls on a tight leader, it will also break. In the throes of excitement it's sometimes difficult to remember to do this—but try anyway. At other times keep a taut line on the fish, never allowing it to rest, and the battle should be over at a rate of about a pound per minute.

On many rivers today, the fighting technique is important because large salmon, those adult fish which are such valuable breeders, must be released. It's much better to fight a fish quickly so it doesn't tire excessively than to prolong the battle and end up with a totally exhausted fish that may not survive even if it is released.

If the fish is a grilse (small salmon) or one that may legally be killed, netting it is the most secure landing method. Netted fish may also be released without undue harm if the fish is not totally lifted from the water or damaged in some other way. If the fish is deeply hooked, simply cut the leader

and sacrifice the fly. Adult salmon may be hand-tailed by grasping them around the muscular "wrist" between tail and body. This requires a sure grip and strong hands but if done correctly will not harm the fish. By holding the tail and supporting the fish beneath the stomach, there's time for "hero" pictures before releasing it.

Atlantic salmon have long been considered a premier species, and anglers have ardently fished for them for centuries. Their supply is limited, thus the reason for conserving the large breeders.

If you plan to release most of the salmon you hook, the leader tippet should be either extremely thin or overly thick. If a 10 pound fish is hooked on a fly attached to a 4-pound-test tippet, a slight jerk will break the leader and free the salmon released. If you want photographs, use a 20-pound tippet, fight the fish quickly and release it as speedily as possible.

An increasing number of Atlantic salmon anglers are fishing with barbless or de-barbed hooks. The barbs can be removed with a three-cornered file or pinched down with pliers or hemostats. If you tie your own, do the un-barbing before you make the fly. Most salmon hooks are strong but brittle and the entire bend of the hook may pop off.

WHAT ARE THE ODDS?

Catching an Atlantic salmon is a major angling thrill and most fly fishermen want to try it. Those who do are usually "hooked" well enough to try it again. Unlike fishing for trout and some Pacific salmon species, success on Atlantics is measured more in hours spent casting than in numbers of fish brought home. On some rivers, catching a fish per day is considered a better than average performance. Any score better than that is outstanding. But—if you have the heart of an angler, it's worth it.

Unless you live close to an Atlantic salmon river or have a pal who does, angling for these elusive fish is mostly done at a recognized salmon camp or lodge. Booking agents, outdoor magazines, and the suggestions of friends are the best sources of information on where to go. Generally, fishing for Atlantic salmon begins in May on the rivers of Maine, June in New Brunswick, Newfoundland, southern Quebec, and Nova Scotia and July and August in northern Quebec and Labrador. Salmon fishing in Iceland and Norway is also a summertime operation. The same holds for Ireland and Great Britain, with the exception of some rivers that see good runs of fish as early as February and March. If you're traveling a great distance, be sure to obtain detailed information beforehand.

TACKLE FOR ATLANTIC SALMON

The basic rod for Atlantic salmon is a 9-footer capable of casting a 9-weight line. This outfit will handle most Atlantic salmon anywhere in the world. For most grilse or small salmon, line sizes 8, 7, or even smaller are adequate, but rods shorter than 8½ are not recommended for beginners. A lot of casting is required on salmon rivers, and to cast for several hours with a short rod is tiring. On some salmon rivers, rods of 10, 12, 14, and 16 feet are quite common, particularly in Great Britain and Norway. It's not that such awesome rods are needed to land the fish, it's merely a matter of casting ease.

Rod length is most often determined by the width of the river or pool being fished. Unless you are a tournament-level caster, its easier to lay out a long line with a long rod than with a short one. Rods of 12 feet or more are usually equipped with grips designed for two-handed use. Europeans have long favored such rods for making what is known as the "spey cast." The spey cast is really a slightly modified roll cast. North American anglers, for one reason or another, prefer one-handed rods and "shoot" long casts by allowing more line to flow through the guides as the rod is driven forward.

A number of rods that are expected to see action on a salmon river are equipped with fighting butts. This can be a permanent extension of two inches or so behind the reel seat or a detachable butt. Detachable models either screw into place or are pushed into place and held there by friction fit. Both work fine when fighting a large fish. The extra length can be used as a hand hold, or braced against the belt or waist as a means of resting the hands.

A fighting butt can be a nuisance when casting if it is fixed. Stray loops of line seem to have a way of wrapping around it. For that reason, I use a detachable butt and keep it in my pocket. When a fish is hooked and makes its initial run, I then snap the butt into place.

A rod that handles large trout well will work nicely for Atlantic salmon. Because most of the angling done for Atlantics will be done with wet flies, a rod that bends more in the middle is the ideal tool. An Atlantic salmon rises to meet a drifting or retrieved wet fly in a distinctive way. It may hold a fly for as long as three or four seconds as it makes its looping move in an attempt to return to the lie. A rod that bends with the fish is a great advantage. It will be a self-hooker 75 percent of the time.

Conversely, if the salmon river requires the use of large dry flies, a stiff, quick-tip sort of action is better suited to handle the extra false casting. A stiff rod will also pick up slack line quicker when it's time to strike.

While all of this presents wonderful excuses for acquiring an extra rod or two, the same advice offered for trout rods applies here as well. A stiff, quick rod can be slowed, or "softened," by using a heavier line. Today's graphite rods are really quite remarkable when called upon to handle different line weights. Graphite rods tend to force a caster to adjust his backcast and forward cast automatically to accommodate the rod's action. This has been proven by rigging identical rods with different line weights and handing the rods to fly casters of average abilities. They quickly adjust their stroke to make the rod perform.

The reel is an important piece of salmon tackle because larger and more active fish are what we're after. When hooked, most salmon make a long, powerful run, and the reel must function smoothly to avoid a break-off. The reel spool should rotate freely and smoothly with just enough drag to slow the fish down a bit but not totally stop it. A 5-pound salmon can break a 10-pound-test leader on its initial run if it's held too tightly. Allowing the fish to run freely against the reel's drag will tire it quickly.

Fly reels are discussed in Chapter 3 and certain makes recommended. With all of this in mind, it's worth repeating that fly reels for Atlantic salmon (and Pacific salmon, too) must be well built and have a large enough spool capacity to hold the fly line and at least 100 yards of backing. Big fish of 20 pounds and up have been known to peel off 250 yards of line. In this case, more is always better than less!

Reels for Atlantic salmon should not only have an adjustable drag feature but the knob or control for it ought to be large enough to find without looking. Ideally, the drag should be preset before fishing commences, but there are times when drag must be tightened or eased when action is taking place. Be sure you know where the drag control is on your salmon reel and how much drag is applied per turn or "click."

While all large fish should be fought from the reel, Atlantic salmon *must* be fought this way or else few of them will be captured. The size and placement of the reel handle is an important detail. The handle should be as close to the edge of the spool as possible and be long enough to grasp easily. Handles mounted on extensions or reels with two handles are nice to look at but can cause all sorts of problems if line gets stuck behind or between them. The fewer protrusions and silhouette oddities the better.

A single handle is also preferred if the angler forgets and has his fingers too close to the rapidly rotating reel spool when a salmon makes a run. There's one less handle to bruise your knuckles!

A floating fly line is the right first choice for Atlantics, with a sink-tip being useful on rare occasions. While I recommend a double-taper fly line for most trout fishing, a weight-forward taper is more suitable for salmon. The longer casts needed and the additional weight of the heavier fly require it.

A tapered leader casts better than a level one. Salmon are not leader shy as are some fussy trout, but a tapered leader helps in presenting the fly. What's needed first is a 30-inch piece of

Reels for Atlantic salmon are similar to those used for trout fishing; they're just larger and hold more line. From left: Scientific Anglers' System 2, Hardy St. John, Cortland Magnum.

25-pound-test material attached to the line with a nail knot. To that heavy butt section, attach 15-inch sections of 20-, 15-, and 12-pound material using blood knots. Finally, tie on a 10-pound tippet about 30 inches long. Precise measurement is not vital—an inch or two, one way or the other, will not matter. The finished leader will measure somewhere between 9 and 10 feet; about the length of the rod. As different flies are tied on and removed the tippet length will become shorter. It's a simple matter to cut off what's left of the 10-pound material and tie on a new tippet.

If you wish to use a lighter tippet, reduce each section by a couple inches and add the new tippet. If a heavier tippet is desired, begin with a 30-pound butt and eliminate the finer tippet. Remember, butt and tippet section should be longer than the other sections. There's plenty of room for minor errors in making tapered leaders for salmon. Most of the time, when casting difficulties arise, it's because the butt section is too short. This is the problem with most of the readymade knotless tapered leaders. The single piece of extruded material changes from thick to thin too quickly. There isn't enough mass to allow the leader to unfurl smoothly. If you use knotless tapered leaders you'll discover they'll cast much better if you add 3 feet of 25-pound-test material to the butt end.

12

Knots

Entire books have been written about knots, and most fishing books contain some information about them. As with many other skills, the rudiments of good knot tying can be learned from studying illustrations, but practice is what counts. Carry a few feet of monofilament line and a fishhook or two with you at all times, and practice on the train, during coffee breaks, at lunch, or any time you have a few spare minutes.

Learning to tie fishing knots quickly and efficiently is fun and guarantees your popularity at a fishing camp because few casual anglers are adept at knot tying. There are only a few knots to learn that are absolutely necessary. Oh, there are

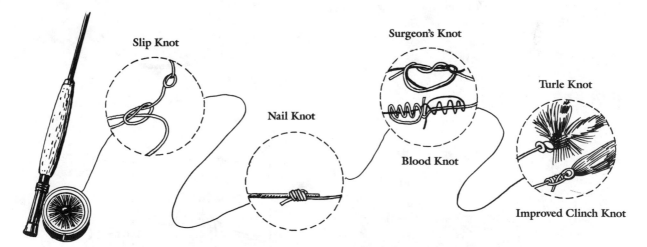

To rig a fly outfit you should know the six knots shown in this diagram. The end of the backing is tied to the reel with a slip knot and an overhand knot is then tied in the end to keep the knot from slipping. The backing is tied to the end of the fly line with a nail knot, and the other end of the line to the leader with another nail knot. Leader sections are tied in with blood knots or surgeon's knots. Finally, the fly is tied to the leader tippet with the improved clinch knot or turle knot.

dozens of intricate ways of joining two strands of line or attaching a hook or lure, but many of these are not as good as the simple ones. Here are the ones you need to know: *improved clinch knot, turle knot, blood knot, surgeon's loop, surgeon's knot,* and *nail knot.* If you are already an accomplished knot tyer or an experienced saltwater angler, you may wonder why some of the more sophisticated line-and-leader connections are not included. The Albright, Bimini twist, spider hitch, and a dozen more are useful at times and it's worthwhile to know how to tie them. But for practical trout and salmon fishing they're not really necessary. Work on the six knots listed until you've got them down pat and most other knots will come easily when you're ready.

Blood Knot

Blood knot is used for joining strands of monofilament to construct a tapered leader. Beginners usually buy knotless leaders at a tackle shop.

Surgeon's Knot

Surgeon's knot is a good substitute for the blood knot and is easier to tie.

Improved Clinch Knot

For trout fishing with spinning or casting tackle, this is the only knot you really need for tying a hook or lure to the end of a monofilament line.

Turle Knot

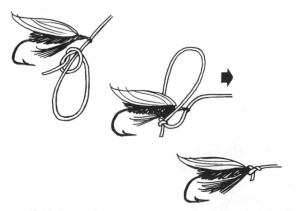

For fly fishing, this is a good alternative to the clinch knot. With it you get a straight pull on the fly.

Surgeon's Loop

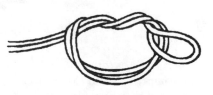

The surgeon's loop is tied in the end of a section of mono that has been tied to the fly line. A leader can then be joined by interlocking the loops.

The nail knot and tube knot are used for tying the butt of the leader to the end of the fly line. These knots make a perfectly straight, thin joint that won't get caught in the rod guides. Most anglers tie a 12-inch section of heavy mono to their fly line with either of these knots, tie a surgeon's loop (below) in the end, and then join the end of the leader to it by interlocking the loops. This system allows you to change leaders in a jiffy.

Nail Knot

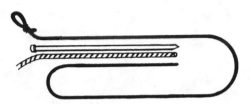

1. *Lay the leader, a finishing nail, and the line side by side, holding them in your left fingers. Then form a large loop, bringing the point of the leader under the line, and grasp it, too, with the left fingers. (Loop is shown much smaller than in actuality.)*

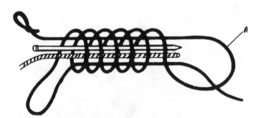

2. *Grasp the loop in the right hand at about point A and wind it around all the strands toward the left hand—about five turns.*

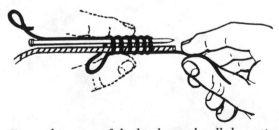

3. *Grasp the point of the leader and pull the entire loop through the coils, holding line, butt, and nail as shown. Then carefully remove the nail, and tighten the knot by pulling on both the butt and the point at the same time.*

Tube Knot

This knot is similar to the nail knot but requires a small plastic tube.

1. *Lay the butt of the leader (shown here without the loop), the fly line, and the tube side by side, holding them in your right fingers.*

2. *Grasp the butt of the leader in your left hand and wind it back around itself, the line, and the tube.*

3. *Thread the end through the tube. Pull the ends of the mono in opposite directions, tightening the coils around the tube.*

4. *Carefully remove the tube and tighten the coils around the line by continuing to pull the ends in opposite directions. Then snip the ends close.*

13

Equipment

In addition to lures, flies, and hooks, a small number of tools should be in every tacklebox and fly-fishing vest.

Clippers

The first and most important of these is some sort of cutting instrument for slicing through monofilament and other line. The cheapest and most efficient are the little nail trimmers that are on display at check-out counters everywhere.

Buy several and scatter them throughout your tacklebox, fishing vest, and pockets. No matter how many you have, you'll never have one too many. They can also be purchased with a little retractable pin-clip that can be attached to your vest or shirt pocket.

Pliers and Forceps

Small pliers or forceps are another must item. They are invaluable for pulling knots tight,

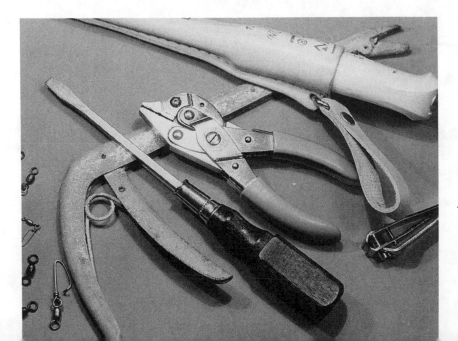

Useful tools for the fisherman: nail clipper, hook disgorger, screwdriver, pliers, filleting knife. Of them all, perhaps the clipper is most important. Use it to cut monofilament and protect your teeth.

removing hooks from fish jaws, pinching on sinkers, straightening bent hooks, and a dozen other chores. Surgical hemostats and needle-holders are wonderful tools; they can be attached to the vest by simply engaging the jaw notches to a pocket. Easily carried in a tacklebox, they can be supplemented with regular pliers or a combination tool such as Leatherman's or a Swiss Army knife.

Some models of the Swiss Army knife are absolute marvels of pocket engineering. At one time or another you'll find a use for every gadget on a Swiss knife. Most anglers consider the scissor feature the most important. Some of the multi-blade models are too heavy for the pocket but are easily carried in a vest.

Knives

The small blade of any pocketknife is all that's needed to clean most trout for the table. It's not necessary to scale small trout since the scales are miniscule. If filleting is called for with larger trout and salmon, a more substantial knife is needed. Thin-bladed filet knives are available in many lengths, styles, and qualities. Some good

ones are sold by Normark, Chicago Cutlery, Case, Western, and the good mail-order houses. Choose one with a fairly soft steel blade that's easy to sharpen. If you're unsure about such things, buy your knife at your local sporting-goods store and ask the clerk to explain the differences among steels. Super-hard blades hold their edge for a long time but are difficult to sharpen. Excessively soft steels are very easy to sharpen but lose their edge in a short time. The ideal fish knife is a compromise of steel composition.

Boots and Waders

The stream and river angler needs foot, leg, and body protection when he's in the water. Depending on the time of year and the temperature of the water, boots and waders not only keep you dry but warm as well. Today's crop of insulated boots (also called "hippers") and waders are wonderfully efficient and durable. Some of them are, however, almost too efficient, and it's easy to become overheated if you do a lot of walking. The best solution is to have two types, insulated and noninsulated. If that's not economically feas-

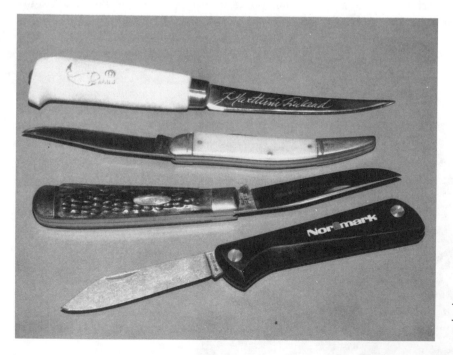

Every angler needs a knife. The bottom three are fold-up models; the top is a Rapala for cleaning small trout. For filleting you'll need a longer blade.

ible, buy the noninsulated kind. Cold days and cold water can be managed with a pair of long johns or wool pants.

All sorts of natural and man-made materials are used in hippers and waders, and anyone would be hard pressed to declare one better than the other. Weight, durability, fit, mobility, style, price are all factors. As expected, some of the most long-lasting fishing footgear is heavy, and some of the most fragile is light in weight. If you spend a lot of time in the water, but don't wade that much, the weight of waders or boots is, of course, less critical than if you're walking a good deal between pools or on dry land.

A popular chest-high wader material among today's anglers is form-fitting Neoprene. Neoprene flexes with body movements and is easy to

Throughout this book you'll notice waders of different styles and materials. Here, international angler Jack Wise is wearing featherweight nylons, great for traveling. Neoprene, Latex, and rubberized canvas all have their advocates. Buy the lightest waders you can find if you perspire easily.

For most trout and salmon fishing, hip boots are sufficient. The most serviceable ones are made of rubber-coated fabric but are heavier too. If weight is a consideration, choose hippers of nylon.

walk in. The lightest boots and waders are those made from coated nylon and designed to be worn with wading shoes. These are called "stocking-foot" waders. The heaviest are rubber or synthetic-coated fabric waders and boots.

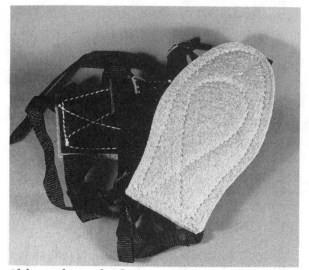

If the waders or hip boots you choose don't have felt soles, by all means acquire some strap-ons. Slippery rocks can end a fishing trip quickly, and being able to wade with confidence means a happier day.

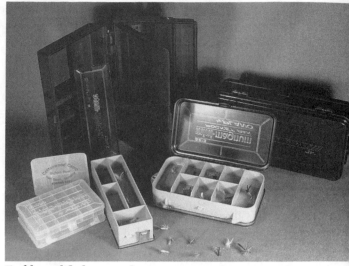

Tackle and fly boxes today are rustproof, waterproof, and nearly unbreakable. This assortment from Plano is a fine example of what's on the market. Forget metal boxes. They rust, they're heavy, and they're out of date.

I've worn many styles and materials over a period of years and all have their advantages. The best plan is to try on different brands and styles for fit and comfort and then think about where and how you're going to use them.

There should be no compromise with the type of sole on boot-foot or stocking-foot hippers and waders. If the stream bottoms you expect to be walking on are rocky, buy *felt soles*. They'll wear out faster than rubber soles, but you'll spend far less time on your backside. If the bottom of your favorite river contains a lot of rounded stones, covered with algae, buy some boot chains or soles with metal cleats or studs. Rubber-soled waders and boots are useful only for hillside walking or on muddy bottoms.

Tackleboxes

There are so many excellent tackleboxes available today that it's almost impossible to pick out the very finest. Unfortunately, there are also a few bargain-basement models that ought to be banned. Almost all makers of quality tackleboxes use moldable plastics that are said to be "high-impact" resistant. Most of them are pretty tough but some aren't. Price is usually the best guide. An examination of the way the box opens, the fit of the trays and compartments, and the sturdiness of the handle and hinges (look for metal) are good clues in determining quality.

There are nearly unlimited sizes, colors, and configurations to choose from among tackleboxes. If you already have a box and are thinking about buying another one, you'll have some idea of how much space you'll need and what size the compartments ought to be. If you're buying your first one, make a survey of your lure and tackle collection and take some measurements. It's annoying to buy a new box and then discover that most of your lures are longer than the individual compartments or vice versa.

Vests

The wading angler needs a vest. Like tackleboxes, these are available in many materials, styles, colors, and pocket counts. A large number of pockets is not necessarily the mark of a good vest. The fly angler wants plenty of pockets, for sure, but the size and placement of the pockets is important. More than one angler has been disappointed on buying a new vest only to discover that his fly boxes, leaders packets, and other gear simply didn't fit the pockets. The best plan is to measure the items you'll be carrying and take a list of measurements to the tackle shop. Selecting the right vest is much easier than having to re-equip with other gear.

All of the mail-order houses that deal in fishing gear carry at least one vest model and some of them offer a half dozen. If you're buying by mail study the photos carefully. Some vests are quite short, designed for the serious wader, while others are almost sport-coat length. Do you like zippers, buttons, snaps, or Velcro strips? Which color? Which material? All of these considerations are highly personal ones and have more to do with style and price than practicality. I like snap fronts because they seem to last longer than zippers or buttons. Bright-colored vests, while pretty in color photos, may cost you a fish or two because fish are not color blind.

Rain Gear

As with most other angling equipment, the choice is wide in the rainwear department. The trend is toward lightweight jackets easily rolled into a small package. A jacket of this sort fits nicely into a fishing vest or boat compartment. Nylon-coated rainwear coated with flexible plastic of some sort dominates the economy range, and more sophisticated materials such as Goretex, and fabric blends treated with Zepel, Scotchgard, and the like (all trade names) are priced considerably higher. As with most things, you get what you pay for. If you expect to be doing a lot of wet-weather fishing don't skimp on quality. On the other hand, if you're a fair-weather angler, a less durable jacket will last a long time.

For boat fishing, rain pants are as important as jackets since it's no fun to sit on a wet backside. Heavier, slicker-type jackets and pants or the rubber-coated variety are also durable and totally waterproof for boat use.

The search for the perfect fishing vest will never end. What's needed is a garment that has enough pockets to hold everything you want to carry. Examine as many vests as possible before buying one.

Rain jackets are essential for wet-weather fishing. Get one with a hood, and with wrist fasteners to prevent water from running up your arms.

14

Caring for and Cooking Your Catch

If you're going to cook or freeze trout or salmon soon after they've been caught, the first thing to do is to remove the gills. These reddish organs are the first to spoil and can taint the meat quickly. Cut through the tissue where the gill covers meet on the bottom of the head. Cut through the arch where the red gills meet at the backbone and the gills will fall away.

If the fish is a trout, slit the belly from vent to throat and push out the entrails with your thumb or forefinger. If you prefer, use a teaspoon. Rinse in cold water and blot dry with a paper towel before cooking.

If the trout are to be frozen, put them into paper milk cartons and fill with water. When frozen in water, small trout will remain firm and good tasting for several months. If the fish to be frozen are too large for milk cartons or other available containers, wrap them tightly in plastic wrap and then double wrap in waxed freezer paper. Try to seal tightly to avoid drying in a frost-free freezer.

Pacific salmon caught in saltwater must be cleaned because they'll have food in their stomachs. Follow the same procedure as with trout. Atlantic salmon caught in freshwater have little or nothing in their stomachs. Remove the gills only; do not remove the entrails or open the body cavity unless you are going to cook the fish within the hour. Double wrap and freeze as you would a large trout. When you decide to eat a frozen Atlantic salmon, allow it to thaw for about three hours and then remove the entrails and wash the body cavity. Everything will come out easily in a semifrozen state.

COOKING FISH

There are times when nearly every rule must be broken, but when cooking fish, the cardinal rule should be chiseled in stone: *Never overcook!*

Sure, we've all heard that admonition, but is there a way to be sure we don't break the rule? There is and it's quite simple. Ten minutes of cooking time (regardless of method) per inch of thickness. The only variable is temperature of the pot, pan, or poacher, which should always be hot enough to cause cooking to begin the instant you introduce the fish. For example, a 1-inch-thick steak or fillet should be fried or broiled no more than 5 minutes on a side. A whole trout or salmon that measures 2 inches at the thickest point should be poached no more than 20 minutes in the bubbling brine. *Note:* The operative words are "no more than," sometimes a bit less time is perfect, and the way to check is to insert a fork at the thickest part of the fish and twist slightly. If the meat is cooked it will flake (come

FILLETING A SALMON OR LARGE TROUT

Spread a couple of layers of newspaper on your work surface and on top place a board a bit longer than the fish. With a sharp filleting knife, cut the fish's head down to the backbone.

Holding the tail firmly in one hand, cut forward from the tail end, running the knife along the backbone.

Apply pressure on the side of the fish with one hand and continue cutting along the backbone until the fillet comes free. Turn the fish, cut the head to the backbone, and remove fillet from other side.

Slip the knife blade under the skin at the tail of the fillet. Holding the skin, cut forward.

The skin will separate from the fillet in one piece.

Slice the flesh just behind the rib bones and remove the bones in one piece. The fillet is now ready for cooking or freezing.

apart) easily and have an opaque appearance instead of a glassy, semitransparent sheen.

TROUT

Frying small trout is a time-honored cooking method. By small, most chefs usually mean fish that are less than 12 or 13 inches long. Fish larger than that don't fit into most household frying pans, but there's another reason: when trout grow beyond that length they tend to become much oilier than the little ones, and don't respond well to frying in fat. Better to broil or poach the larger ones.

Plain Fried Trout

Wipe the fish dry with a paper towel and roll them in all-purpose flour until they are fully

CLEANING A SMALL TROUT

Hold the trout belly up and insert the tip of the knife into the gill opening. Cut the tissue where the gill covers meet the bottom of the head, then cut through the arch where the red gills meet at the backbone.

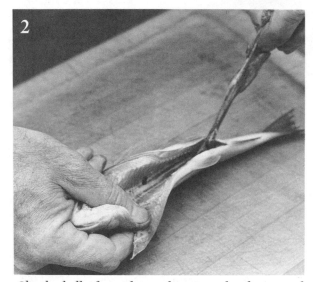

Slit the belly from the anal vent to the throat and pull out the gills and innards in one piece.

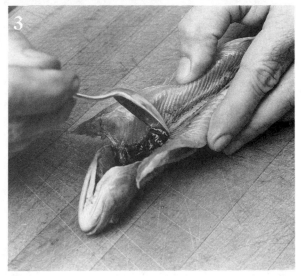

With a spoon, clean out remaining blood from the cavity and rinse quickly under cold water. Blot dry with a paper towel. The trout is now ready for cooking or freezing.

dusted. Preheat a heavy skillet (cast iron is best) with a mixture of one half margarine and one half butter. Use enough to cover the bottom of the skillet so that it bubbles over the entire surface. Lay the fish in the skillet evenly and salt and pepper lightly—you can always add more at the table to suit individual tastes. Fry for three minutes on one side, turn them and fry for about the same amount of time on the other. Check for doneness and remove immediately to a warmed plate lined with a double layer of paper towels. Allow the fat to soak into the towel for a minute and serve with lemon wedges.

Variations on this basic method include using prepared bread crumbs, cornmeal, powdered saltines or crushed cereal instead of the flour. If you prefer not to use butter, almost any kind of cooking oil can be substituted. Because it was available, I suppose, bacon fat was a popular cooking fat in the early days of fish frying. Some people still use it, but it tends to alter the taste of fresh trout. To know what fresh fried trout really tastes like, stick with a less pungent form of fat.

Poaching Trout

Poaching is cooking fish in boiling water . . . not a rolling boil but a slowly bubbling boil. It is the purest and easiest method of cooking whole or pieces of fish and the best one for those who are serious about watching calories. Any sort of pot, roaster, or large skillet will do the job. Add enough water to the utensil to cover the fish and bring it to a mild boil. Add a few peppercorns, a stalk of celery, and an onion if you like and simmer for five minutes or so. Add the fish and cook for that magic "ten minutes per inch." With small, whole trout, which won't measure an inch thick, a couple of minutes less will be plenty. Remove with a spatula and serve.

For an elegant presentation, you may want to skin the fish before serving. Nothing to it. Use a table fork to lift the cooked skin from each side. It will slide off easily. Garnish with lemon slices, fresh tomato, or cucumber and your guests will think they're at a 5-star restaurant. The same treatment can be applied to fillets or steaks from larger fish.

Broiled Trout

Here again, whole fish, fillets, or steaks may be used. Brush each side with butter or cooking oil and lay the fish on top of a broiler rack that's been covered with aluminum foil. Salt lightly and preheat the broiler. Cook the required time (remember the rule) on one side and then the other. Serve with fish sauce or citrus wedges. *Tip:* Turn the fish with a *warmed* spatula to avoid sticking. Read on for sauce recipes.

Baking Trout

Trout less than 13 inches are too small to bake,

but the oven will do a splendid job with those 15 inches or longer. Use a shallow baking dish or a foil-lined cookie sheet. Salt and pepper to taste and oil on both sides. Preheat the oven to 400 degrees and bake for the required ten minutes per inch. If the fish is a thick one, sprinkle a layer of bread crumbs on the top side to prevent excessive browning of the skin or outer layer of flesh. The fish may also be wrapped in aluminum foil. Reduce heat.

From these basic methods just about every great fish recipe has its beginnings. The variations and nuances merely require the addition of extra flavors added while the fish is cooking or the application of condiments and sauces. The squeezing of lemon, lime, or orange juice on fish is an accepted habit almost world wide and appeals to most tastes.

In English-speaking countries, the application of tartar sauce is also a common practice. Tartar sauce, if not excessively used, is good with trout and salmon, but the ubiquitous tomato-based "seafood sauce" is not recommended by most trout lovers. Trout, especially the small ones which most of us cook, are too delicate in flavor to stand up to the horseradish and spicy additions in many of these sauces.

SALMON

Salmon from the Atlantic or Pacific are never at their best when fried. Some cooks do fry them, but there is far too much natural oil in salmon to be served well by cooking them in still more fat.

Because most salmon spend part of their lives in saltwater and part of it in freshwater, we catch them in various condition "levels." Put another way, some of them carry a lot of fat between the layers of flesh and some don't. Generally, a fish caught in saltwater will be fatter or more oily. Very oily fish respond better to poaching or outside grilling because the oil "floats" off in the hot water or drips off when grilled over wood coals or charcoal. Baking or broiling is ideal for fish that have been in freshwater for a month or longer. Fish that are more silvery in color are usually the fatter ones.

The "ten minute per inch thickness rule" applies with salmon just as it does with trout. All of the recipes and cooking techniques listed for trout apply with salmon with the possible exception of broiling. Salmon, because of their extra oil, can stand a bit more broiling time but be sure to check the texture of the flesh often. When the full thickness of the steak, fillet, or whole fish takes on a uniform pinkish tone it's probably done.

Poached salmon

There is no more elegant meal in this world than a whole poached salmon. The major problem this presents to fish chefs is finding the proper utensil of the right size. Most Atlantic salmon of the grilse category are about 24 inches long. Fortunately, that precise length seems to be a standard size for fish poaching pans. If a salmon is longer than that it must be beheaded or cut in two in order to fit. Larger fish poachers are available but difficult to find in most stores in America. However, kitchen specialty shops will be happy to order one for you.

Fish poachers are made from tin, aluminum, copper, or stainless steel and are sold at various price levels. Almost all of them come with a perforated rack that lifts the entire fish out of the pan when cooking is completed. If you poach the fish in a poultry roasting pan, wrap the fish in cheesecloth so it can be lifted out without breaking in two.

The actual poaching is very simple. Run enough water into the pan to cover the fish. You can check this by inserting the fish into the cold water. Remove the fish and heat the water to a gentle boil. As the water is bubbling add a stalk of celery, a scraped carrot cut into chunks, one peeled onion, a bay leaf, a handful of peppercorns, a teaspoon of salt, and a cup of dry vermouth. Allow these ingredients to boil for 20 minutes and then insert the fish. When the water begins to bubble again, allow it to cook for 20 minutes and check by thrusting a toothpick into the thickest part. If it penetrates easily, the fish is done. If not, cook for 2 minutes more and turn off the heat.

Lift the fish out by picking up the rack (if using a poacher) or grasp the ends of the cheesecloth bag and lay the fish on several layers of newspaper. Skin the top side of the fish with a dull table knife—the skin will scrape off cleanly. Remove the eye from the socket. Now, carefully slip a pair of spatulas underneath the whole fish and slide it onto a fish platter of the right size or a cookie sheet. If the fish isn't overcooked and you move swiftly and positively, the fish won't fall apart; if it does, you must patch it back together for a nice appearance.

Garnish the edge of the serving dish with fresh lettuce, parsley, or watercress. Slice wedges of lemon, tomato, or perhaps green and red peppers for additional decoration on top of the fish, and pop an olive into the eye socket.

Serve a poached salmon by inserting the edge of a large fork or spatula into the lateral line that is plainly visible on each side of the skinned and cooked fish. The meat will easily pull away from the ribs, which remain attached to the backbone. When the meat from one side has been served, turn the fish over for the next helping.

The sauces listed for trout are all excellent with salmon, particularly the dill sauce.

American Fish Boil

An offshoot of poaching is the fish boil. Different versions of this outdoor favorite have taken form over the years but they're all basically the same. A fish boil requires chunks of fatty trout or salmon, potatoes, and onions. Other vegetables, such as carrots, celery, turnips, cabbage, and what have you can be added if those flavors suit the palette. All that's needed is a large pot, screen basket, or colander and a rack over the fire to set the pan on.

Here's how to do it for four hungry eaters:

6 quarts of water in an 8-quart (or larger) kettle.
8 peeled potatoes about the size of a baseball.
4 large onions
6 large carrots split in half
2 cups of celery chunks
1 cup of salt
two teaspoons of pepper

A handsome salmon ready to be poached. In the poacher, cold water seasoned with vegetables and herbs and simmered for twenty minutes to develop flavor. The salmon is immersed in the boiling liquid by lowering the rack. Roasting pan can also be used for poaching large fish.

3 pounds of fish steaks cut 2 inches thick

Bring the water to a rolling boil. Drop the basket with all ingredients except the fish into the water. Add the salt and pepper and cook for 15 minutes when the water boils again. Add the fish steaks to the basket and cook an additional 15 minutes. Lift the basket out and serve with melted butter and homemade bread.

Note: This is an especially good method to use with salmon or lake trout from the Great Lakes. Be sure to leave the skin on the steaks in order to prevent the meat from falling apart. If salmon are used, scale first.

Broiled Salmon

Salmon, east or west, are wonderful when broiled. Beginning with the basic method all sorts of sauces and prepared condiments can be added before or after. Fillets or steaks can be broiled with or without skin attached. It's difficult to broil thin fillets correctly. Pieces of fish at least an inch and no more than 2 inches thick are perfect.

Cover the broiling rack with heavy aluminum foil. Grease the foil and set oven to "broil" or 550 degrees. Broil for five minutes on one side, turn and apply a dab of butter or margarine (or other flavorings or sauce) and cook for another five minutes. Check for doneness.

Various kinds of prepared mustards are great on broiled salmon and a favorite is French's Dip & Spread. After turning the fish, spread a thin coating on top and continue the cooking. The mustard will brown nicely and protect the fish from overcooking.

If you enjoy devising new sauces, just remember that small fish are delicately flavored whereas larger fish have a more pronounced "fishy" flavor and use pungent spices accordingly.

Baked Salmon

Aluminum foil is the most important "utensil" for baking salmon. The fish should be loosely wrapped or "tented" in foil to avoid excessive drying or burning. Simply add the flavors wanted or just salt, pepper, and a dab of butter, and bake ten minutes per inch of thickness—but never for more than thirty minutes at 400 degrees without checking. When the fish flakes easily at the backbone, it's done.

Smoking Trout and Salmon

The earthy, outdoorsy taste of smoked fish is popular with most anglers, and it's easy to prepare at home. All you need is one of the box-type aluminum smokers sold by Luhr Jensen or Outers. Soak the fillets, steaks, or whole fish in a saltwater brine for ten hours, dry, and pop in the smoker for six to eight hours. Instructions that come with each smoker are easy to follow and the results will be delicious. I've been using these little electric smokers for decades and have yet to find any system that does it better.

As with any kind of fish cookery, check often for doneness. It's especially important when smoking since the "rule" doesn't apply here. Smokers must be used outside, so the variable of air temperature makes precise timing difficult. If the air temperature is 75 degrees, for example, fish may be well smoked within four or five hours. If it's zero, a full eight hours may be required.

Gravlox, or Salt-cured Fish

The Scandinavian specialty, Gravlox, is easy to make if you begin three days in advance. When served with fresh lemon or lime juice on a crisp cracker there is no finer appetizer.

½ cup coarse salt
½ cup sugar
1 tablespoon dill weed
1 tablespoon fresh ground pepper
5 to 7 pound salmon or large trout, filleted

Fillet a salmon or large trout, after scaling and dust the flesh sides with a mixture of salt, sugar, dill weed, and coarse black pepper. Press the flesh sides together, matching them as they came from the fish. Place the matched sides in a glass or ceramic dish and put a board or stack of old magazines on top of them. Weight this down with a couple of bricks or a sack of sugar and set in the refrigerator for three days. The object is to press out as much oil as possible and allow the salt and sugar to penetrate the flesh. Inspect once a day and remove the oil that is squeezed out. Blotting with paper towels is the easiest way of doing this.

After three days, scrape off the crusted salt and sugar and wipe with a damp towel. Slice from either end of the fillet as thinly as possible. The leftover fillet may be wrapped in foil and kept (well chilled) for another two weeks.

SAUCES

The sauce recipes that follow are family favorites and have been altered over the years by my favorite fishing companion and cookbook author, wife Sylvia.

Cucumber Sauce

1 cup sour cream
1 tablespoon fresh dill weed
¼ cup minced cucumber
1 teaspoon minced onion
½ teaspoon dry mustard
1 teaspoon chervil or parsley
Dash of salt and pepper

Mix all ingredients in ceramic bowl and chill for an hour.

Dill Sauce

This is our favorite salmon sauce, but it goes just as well with large trout.

1 cup mayonnaise
¼ cup prepared mustard
1 teaspoon lemon juice
1 teaspoon steak sauce
½ teaspoon dill weed
¼ teaspoon salt

Mix well and chill for an hour.

Hot Wine Sauce

½ cup dry vermouth
1 tablespoon minced onion
¼ teaspoon crushed tarragon
1½ tablespoons butter
1 tablespoon minced parsley
Dash of salt

Combine all ingredients in saucepan except butter and parsley and bring to a low boil. Add the butter and parsley and serve over poached or broiled trout.

Tomato Sauce

½ package dried tomato soup mix
   (about an ounce)
1 cup sour cream
2 tablespoons chopped green pepper
⅓ cup medium sherry

Heat all ingredients to just below boiling point and serve.